No Liver
No Shoes

The story of how God changed a whole community
and taught them the only way to live is
TRUSTING ONLY JESUS ALWAYS!!!

By
Sarah Wright

RM Rochester Media

Published by:
Rochester Media, Inc
PO Box 80002
Rochester, MI 48308
248-429-READ (7323)
248-430-8799 fax
info@rochestermedia.com
www.rochestermedia.com

All scripture quotations, unless otherwise indicated, are taken from Holy Bible, New International Version NIV R (Reserved Symbol?) copyright C (Copyright Symbol?) 1973, 1978, 1984 by International Bible Society.

Author: Sarah Wright
Edited by Sarah L. Hovis
Formating by Brian Jamieson

First U.S. Edition Year 1st Edition was Published

Publisher's Cataloging-In-Publication Data

Sarah Wright

No Liver No Shoes
Summary: The story of how God changed a whole community and taught them the only way to live is

13 Digit ISBN 978-1461063018

Christian Living, Spiritual Growth, Christianity, Religion

For current information about releases by Sarah Wright from Rochester Media, Inc., visit our web site: http://www.rochestermedia.com

Printed in the United States of America

Acknowledgements

There was a time that the idea of me writing this page in a book which I had authored would have been inconceivable. Then again, I never imagined that at forty-five I would be a widow. But, as this life would have it, here I am. Most importantly, I didn't know that losing someone so special in my life would lead me closer to God. But, praise the Lord, it did.

Let me begin by thanking God for being my life-line and for being faithful to me and my children in this process. God's goodness and faithfulness brought me out of darkness and into His marvelous light.

To my Friday morning bible study ladies, I couldn't have done it without you. The time it took to go through this journey was incredibly healing and filled with laughter, tears and the true joy of Jesus. God showed us the way. I am so grateful we had the courage and heart to follow.

To my children, Amy and Ben, how your hearts and lives have been changed since July 3, 2004; when your father was called home by his maker. The love shared between you and dad was and continues to be ever present in your lives. Follow his lead and keep running to God, whose arms are open, waiting for you to come and trust and love.

To the members of King of Kings Lutheran Church, Lake Orion, MI, thank you for your love and great mercy. Thank you for being the Body of Christ and showing God's great goodness and love during a time when we all had to try and find our way. You were a true blessing to Luther, Amy, Ben and I, going far above what we thought possible. But like Luther said, 'There is nothing too beautiful or impossible for God to do. God showed that so vividly through you. Thank you.

To Kim and Tara and Christine who have worked and reworked this book into what it is today. Your gifts and talents are many. Your faithful following of your Lord shines through every page of this book. Thank you for your love for me and my family and Luther but, most of all, for Jesus Christ. You are wonderful examples of God's love, grace and mercy. Thank you for allowing God to use you as His instruments. The music of your hearts is beautiful.

No Liver
No Shoes

The story of how God changed a whole community
and taught them the only way to live is
TRUSTING ONLY JESUS ALWAYS!!!

By
Sarah Wright

Table of Contents

Introduction

We thought we were taking care of Luther. As I look back, he was actually taking care of us.

In this book, I narrate on a collection of inspirational emails and letters from physicians and loved ones that were exchanged over the two-year period during my husband, Luther's, journey with cancer. They have been compiled to share with you our voyage with Jesus, in the light and in the darkness.

Luther L. Wright, first and foremost a child of God, was my husband for 24 years. He was a devoted father to our two children, Amy, age 18 and Ben, age 15. He was also a brother, son, friend, spiritual guide, mentor, funny man, pastor and follower of Jesus Christ.

He taught me many things, but the most wonderful was T.O.J.A. – Trust Only Jesus Always. He believed it, lived it, walked it and talked it. As you follow with us on this journey, I pray you will see what I saw. God showed Himself to Luther so vividly on this earth, allowing him to share Christ's glory with those he was leaving behind as he prepared to join Jesus in heaven. God revealed Himself to us, demonstrating His endless love, grace, mercy and provision in the most difficult time of our lives. Only then could we run and tell others, you, what He did for us. What He can do and what He will do for you.

Chapter 1

Thanksgiving

"Do not be anxious about anything, but in everything, by prayer and petition, with thanksgiving, present your requests to God." Philippians 4:6

What will win? The spread of cancer or movement up the transplant list? This question ran over and over again in our minds.

My husband needed a new liver and new running shoes. He had been an avid runner for 25 years and I begged him to get new shoes because his were past the point of embarrassment. His response: "No liver, no shoes." We were told the wait for a new liver would be one year or more. Could we really wait that long for a liver or new shoes? Sometimes we forget that God is always and forever in control, no matter the outcome.

I learned many things during this process. For example, my husband was not a person whose glass was half full or half empty. He saw it as full when it was empty. He would have days of despair and fear and sadness, but they did not last long.

Luther would sit at the computer for three to four hours, writing and re-writing until his words read exactly how he wanted them to. When he sat to write an email, he was actually processing his thoughts and feelings. As a

Pastor he loved to preach and teach and his e-mails were a mixture of preaching, teaching and processing.

He always had a message of hope and praise. He often said, "when you go into the Word, the Bible, you never come out the same as when you entered into it." I saw that happen time and time again as he would write and tell his story. He loved to tell THE story of Jesus and His love. That is apparent in all of his writings.

Thoughts and thanksgiving from Luther's physician. August 4, 2005

Leonard G. Quallich, III, M.D.
Center for Digestive Health
Gastroenterologist

Dear Sarah,

Thank you for the opportunity to convey to you some of my thoughts during Luther's journey. It is a rare occurrence that a physician can provide this type of information to a patient and family. Usually, after the loss of a loved one, people try to "move on" and forget what transpired. I clearly understand this motivation and would likely try to do the same. However, this would be a missed opportunity to share with you what an incredible privilege it was to care for your husband. I found him to be one of the kindest, compassionate and most gentle souls I have ever met. I learned so much from him as a person and as a physician. Luther helped me find continued meaning in my work that has helped sustain me and my other patients. But first, let's start at the beginning...

I met Luther my first day at Beaumont Hospital. It was a pretty hectic day, running all around the hospital caring for quite sick patients. I performed Luther's procedure that day and recall being surprised at the results. He had a stricture in his bile duct. Based on the x-rays and location of the stricture, I knew this could really be only one diagnosis-cancer. Luther was so young for this diagnosis, but I knew what the results meant. I hate this part of my job. Telling someone young that they have a terminal diagnosis is obviously not an easy task. Unfortunately, I have done this quite a lot. It is difficult not to put yourself in your patient's place. What if this was me or a family member? How would I react? What would I do? It is not fair. Luther did nothing wrong. He didn't make this happen. He couldn't have prevented it. Yet here we are. I remember impressions from that day. I remember the support of his family, the willingness to fight this and stick together. I know this would be a long, difficult journey, but at least he wasn't going to do this alone.

Things progressed. Luther went to the Mayo clinic, underwent treatments and had done well for awhile. I remember many things from those visits. What I was impressed with the most was the hope. Not a false hope, nothing unrealistic. Just the hope to enjoy a single day and enjoy what life had to offer. From my perspective, Luther lived every day; he didn't just exist like so many of us do. He understood the value of time; time with family, time with friends. He would talk about his kids, baseball games and plans for tomorrow. In the face of a terminal diagnosis, Luther had the grace and courage to live for today and hope for tomorrow.

I learned a great many other things from Luther during this time as well. Luther reminded me why I went to medical school in the first place. I love taking care of patients. I love the interactions with patients and families. Many times we as physicians forget this along the way. Insurance companies, the threat of frivolous lawsuits, busy schedules, time away from family, running the business side to a practice, charts, charts and more charts to complete all conspire to make us forget why we are here in the first place. It is easy to just show up and forget the joy that drew many of us into medicine. No matter how busy I was, nor how far behind I was in my schedule, I always looked forward to seeing you and Luther in the office. From his smart alec grin to the constant grief about Michigan's football team, I always had a smile on when you came for visits. Luther's sense of humor was infectious. Even now when I think of Luther, I still smile about all of the grief he would give me and how great his sense of humor was. I think of that all of the time now. When things are extra busy or I am tired of all of the hassles of medicine, I remember Luther. I remember the joy I have taking care of patients. I remember why I went to medical school. This lesson has truly helped me personally and I try and share that love of medicine with my new patients. I will always be grateful for that.

As things approached the end, I remember the grace and selflessness of Luther. He understood the nature of his terminal disease. I never saw him lash out or being hateful because of the cancer. I would have understood if he wanted to scream at how unfair this was. Rather, he did as he always did when I knew him. He lived for today and accepted things with a quiet dignity that is unparallel in my experience. Luther also impressed upon me the importance of his family. He wanted to spend as much quality time as possible with you and the children. Seeing the kids at their sporting events was so important to him. He wanted to be well for you. We talked many times when he was in the hospital. The only thing that seemed to matter was to get well enough to go home to be with you and the children.

In the end, I find that I have gained more than I could have possibly given back. I tried my very best as a physician to help you and Luther. When there was nothing more I could do, I tried to at least be there for you and your family during this journey. Even so, I find that I received so much more than I could give. I learned about grace and dignity from the greatest of teachers. I learned about hope and compassion. I learned about humor and joy even in the setting of personal tragedy. I was reminded what a genuine privilege it is to be a physician. I try every single day to remember these lessons so I may help my patients. For that I will be eternally grateful. Thank you, Luther.

Sincerely,

Leonard Quallich, M.D.

Chapter 2

How Our Journey Began

"But as for me and my house we will serve the
Lord." Joshua 24:15b

It was September 1978; our junior year at Capital University in Columbus Ohio. Ironically, I went back to college that summer thinking, "I'm not going to date anyone." I was just going to college to hang with my friends. I had just broken up with a boyfriend and wasn't really in the mood for going through all that again.

My friend Mary Jo and I were sitting in class when in walked two boys who caught both of our attention. Fortunately, we weren't looking at the same boy.

Luther lived near the beach in Florida and had worked construction that summer, so he was very tanned. He had long blonde hair and was quiet and shy. I was thinking to myself, "Who is this new boy?" It never crossed my mind that I would date a boy with long hair, especially since I don't like it. Luther may have been shy, but I, on the other hand, was a pretty outgoing person. Mary Jo and I would get to class early to strategically arrange the seats. She would sit by Mark and I would sit by Luther.

I'll never forget the first time I got 'the look.' We were all four in the cafeteria and as we walked by Luther tilted his head toward me and gave me this look as our eyes locked together. Mary Jo said to me, "I think he likes you." It was a look I saw many times during our marriage.

Our dating was pretty gradual over the year. We double dated with Mary Jo and Mark most of the time. Our first date, just the two of us, was out to dinner and then back to the dorm to watch television. That night it took Luther about two hours to decide if he should kiss me good night, so I took the initiative and kissed him. We both floated back to our rooms that evening.

We had only been dating a few months when I took Luther home to meet my parents. My dad, a Lutheran pastor, was out working in the yard in his jean overalls. Luther decided to go outside and chat with him for awhile. My dad said to Luther, "Where I come from, if you have long hair, they think you are a drug dealer." When Luther returned inside he took me into the bathroom and told me what my dad said about his hair. He was mortified.

In spite of his hair, Luther was able to win dad over. While I was unpacking my things, dad came into my bedroom and said to me, "You finally found him. You finally found Mr. Right". Summer came and Luther returned home to Florida and I to Ohio. We talked on the phone and he wrote to me every day. Luther flew out for my brother's wedding and when my brother, his fiancée and I picked Luther up from the airport, he gave me 'the look' again. It was late when we got home. I remember driving up to the house and thinking 'mom and dad were waiting for us?' When we got in the house dad had terrible news. Luther's father had a heart attack. His dad, Don, kept telling Jean, Luther's mom, not to tell Luther. He didn't want him to have to come home. By the next day Luther's dad had another heart attack. Luther left immediately after the wedding. As we sat in the airport we talked of an engagement.

Our next talk of engagement was later that summer in Florida. We were sitting on the beach and Luther told me that he had bought me an engagement ring, but had returned it. He needed the money for college. He didn't want to burden his parents with tuition fees. Luther asked if I would be willing to accept an opal for the time being. Of course I said yes. With each month that passed, I anxiously awaited for the ring. Month after month went by and no ring showed up. By the time January rolled around I came to the conclusion that he had changed his mind. It was January 2nd and we were in the car traveling to visit his sister. Luther unexpectedly pulled into a truck stop and parked between two semis. He pointed to the glove compartment and said, "Go ahead and open it." There was the ring box. He asked if I wanted to open it. Setting my frustration aside, I realized this was the moment. Naturally, I said yes.

Our wedding was simple. We were married at my dad's church in Ohio. Dad was nervous walking me down the aisle, but remained steady as a rock. My brother Steve, also a pastor, did the beginning of the ceremony and Dad finished. That day, I knew I had never been sure of anything in my life. I felt calm and joyful. The reception was in the church basement. We were married at 2:30 in the afternoon. By 5 p.m., Luther was changed and ready to leave. I was still mingling and loving every moment. He stood at the top of the steps calling down to me, "Are you ready to go?" I changed and off we went.

Our first year of marriage was very good. We lived in Columbus in my grandmother's house. She was living with my parents by then. I was a social worker at a local hospital and Luther was working at a call-in crisis center. During that year he actively looked for opportunities for graduate school. We had decided on Florida State University. He wanted to get his Master's in Social Work, studying Research and Policy. I was at work one day when he called to ask if getting a full scholarship and a monthly stipend would be helpful. It was one of those 'laugh out loud' moments at how God does provide. Two months later we were at FSU.

We attended the Lutheran campus church there. The pastor was a young family man who made quite an impression on Luther and me. Luther was working at a mental health agency when he realized that it is difficult to treat the whole person without the spiritual element involved. As we attended church and met with the pastor, Luther decided, with the guidance of God, to go onto seminary and become a pastor himself. Having grown up as a pastor's daughter, I had always said I would never marry a pastor. Never say never. Luther was a social worker when we got married. I like how God works in our lives in spite of us.

Luther received his MSW in 10 months and then moved onto Trinity Lutheran Seminary. He felt a strong calling to inner city ministry and began pursuing it. I, on the other hand, had some struggling to do with the idea of inner city ministry. During our time at Trinity, we went on two different weekend experiences in Pittsburg and Cincinnati to get an idea of what this calling meant. As time went on, God worked on my heart and I could see Luther's passion. Our third year was an internship in Denver. Amy, our daughter, was three months old at the time. We lived in a low-income, high-rise apartment building on the 6th floor. Our bedroom overlooked downtown Denver and Mile High Stadium. The living room looked out over the mountains. It was beautiful. I felt safe and I felt confident that I -we-could do inner city ministry. Looking back, I now realize that this was a great stepping stone in God, easing me into Luther's next call to Detroit.

We arrived in Detroit in 1986. We were excited to have reached the goal of serving God in the city. I was three months pregnant with our second child, Ben. Truth Lutheran's congregation was a people of great faith who were struggling through the city's transition from European American traditionalism to a now African American community. Among their trials was the desire to reflect and minister to their neighbors in need. Luther soon became known as an activist for peace and justice, speaking out for those who couldn't speak, 'For the least of them', for those who got overlooked. For those whom Jesus had come to save. Luther thrived in the inner-city. He was very bold, taking a stand and marching to rid the neighborhood of the many drug houses.

We soon found out the Denver inner-city and the Detroit inner-city weren't the same at all. We lived on the corner across the street from the church and a middle school. Everyone knew where the pastor lived. City ministry was 24/7. People were knocking on the door in the middle of the night, the windshield was blown out of our car, crisis of every kind and constant turmoil, it seemed. I remember coming home and searching the house before entering, the gunfire every night, the church alarm going off in the middle of the night and Luther running over there alone. It was intense living like that everyday. As frightening and extreme as it was, there was energy to living in crisis all the time.

Ben was born in February and a week later Luther had to leave to be with his dad who was having surgery. There I was with a three year old and a one week old baby, alone in the house for seven days. We tried to get someone to stay with me, but it was too hard for people. Their fears of where we lived were great.

After nine years in the city, I had a breakdown. Amy wouldn't go outside to play without us. She didn't even like me to take the trash out by myself. It took me two years to tell Luther how I felt. I wanted to protect him and the kids while supporting his 70 to 80 hour work weeks. I was torn between the hardship and the great love and compassion I had for the people we had come to know and live among. Then, one Sunday, I crashed. There I lay on the floor for four hours thinking I should get up and care for my family, but my body refused to move. I was paralyzed emotionally. It was then we knew we had to make a change.

I remember Luther going to the Board to talk to them about moving. He knew we needed to go. He didn't want to live in the suburbs and do ministry in the city. However, Truth Church was not ready for us to leave. The church rented us a house in Royal Oak, a city outside of Detroit. I knew how difficult this was for Luther. To move out of the city and continue ministry in the city just didn't feel right to him. But for me and his family, he was willing to do it. I was in such a black hole of depression, still struggling with this decision and wondering if it was the right thing to do.

Then one day, as Ben was outside in the back lot playing basketball with his friends, a man pulled out a gun and shot it. My son came running to the house terrified. It was time to move. Our decision was confirmed. My prayer the day we left our home in Detroit was that it would be a smooth and easy move. However, it was the worst move of our lives. Luther was beside himself with anger, frustration and pain. The most difficult was when neighborhood people came by asking why we were leaving. I saw his heart break each time. And yet, I knew we were moving because of Luther's love for me and the kids. Once settled in Royal Oak, Luther was depressed for six months. I must say how grateful I was to people of Truth Church and their love and understanding in what was an extremely difficult situation. Royal Oak was three years of healing and grace.

After some time, Luther began interviewing with other inner-city churches. None of them were just right. God threw us a curve ball with a call to a church 45 minutes north of Detroit in Lake Orion, Michigan. King of Kings Lutheran Church. When asked to interview, he wondered what they would see in him. He was a city pastor at heart and did not feel he would fit into the suburban church. What he found was what they saw in him, the love and grace of Jesus Christ.

Royal Oak had been a great bridge before getting to Lake Orion. Ben, however, age 7, was angry with us for two years. He had many friends in Royal Oak, and all close enough to ride his bike. Once in Lake Orion, he had to be driven to his friends. He was used to playing sixteen hours a day, riding his bike to and from everywhere, and was now confined on a certain level. Amy, age 10, adjusted easily to the move.

King of Kings was a church we were familiar with. They were mission partners with Truth. They accepted us with arms wide open. As they were putting Luther's financial package together, they noticed we had only one car and it was old and rusted. Next thing we knew, they were leasing us a mini van. The day we went to pick it up, Luther and I just sat in it for awhile in awe. I was so excited. I had wanted a mini van for nearly a decade. We were overwhelmed by the generosity.

Chapter 3

Awe-full

**"Trust in the Lord with all your heart and lean not on
your own understanding." Proverbs 3:5**

The first days of the cancer diagnosis were
overwhelming and frightening. All of a sudden we were
living on a fast and furious roller coaster. Luther began
having symptoms of severe abdominal pain on June 14,
2002, our twenty-second wedding anniversary. He described
it as a bowling ball on fire going in through his chest and
out his back. On July 3rd Luther had an ERCP, a procedure
to look at the bile duct area. As I waited for Dr. Quallich
to come out with news of a probable bile duct stone, my
daughter Amy came to sit with me and to visit her dad. I
was thankful we were together as Dr. Q escorted us into a
conference room where he gave us the shocking news of
an inoperable, incurable, rare cancer, cholangiocarcinoma,
cancer of the bile ducts.

When he left the room, I sat with Amy in disbelief.
I began feeling this tremendous weight, a sick ache in my
gut, and thinking my 18-year-old had just heard her father
has cancer with no hope of cure. I looked at her and she
at me, our eyes filled with sadness and fear. Panic was in
her voice when shc said, "This can't be happening, Dad
and I just started to get along again." You know those years

of teenage-ness when parents and their children constantly battle? That was us with her in high school. Things had just started to calm down some and Luther and I could actually have a conversation with her without an argument. As we sat in that conference room, after hearing the news of Luther's cancer, she realized immediately what it all meant. How could I begin to comfort her? What could I do or say to help her when I was feeling the same panic and disbelief as she? Amy sobbed, trying to grapple with the worst news of her young life. I held her. I don't believe I said much; 'I love you' was all I had to offer.

It felt as if a black hole had just opened and we were being swallowed up by it. After an hour of trying to console her, we went to Luther's room where he was still heavily medicated. Amy left to go home to get our son, Ben, to bring him to the hospital.

I called David, Luther's brother and a physician, with the news. I could tell by the sound of his voice that the situation was not good. The next morning, just after Luther awoke and learned of the tumor, David and his wife Cindy walked in. Luther was thrilled to see them, but just as quickly realized how serious it must be for David to leave his practice and come so quickly. Soon after Luther's brother, Don, arrived with his wife, Carol Ann, from New Jersey.

That afternoon the doctor came in to say that the tests confirmed the cholangiocarcinoma and there was little hope. We cried for some time. With all of us gathered together in that small hospital room, Luther began ministering to us as he always did. He shared with us the psalms he was led to read that morning. Psalms 118:8, "It is better to take refuge in the Lord then to put confidence in mortals" and Psalms 130:6, "My soul waits for the Lord more than those who watch for the morning." I marveled at his faithfulness in God whom he obviously trusted so completely.

Later that day, Dr. Q came in to tell us more details of the cancer…no cure…does not respond well to radiation or chemo…four to seven months to live. I wept as I had never done before. It came from the deepest part of my soul. Fear, panic, sadness, loss, oh dear God, what do we do now? Luther was the love of my life. Yes, we had hills and valleys in our life together, but many more high hills than low valleys. And in the valleys we grew a closer and deeper love for each other which made the hilltops even more beautiful.

There we were, all together in that room, scared, lost, afraid, but not alone. God was with us. Just at that moment, He sent the Bishop from the Evangelical Lutheran Church of America into the room and we prayed. What else could we do? For us, trusting only Jesus always really began that day, that very minute. Where else could we go? To whom else could we turn? Jesus. Yes, Jesus.

That night Luther's mom, Jean, arrived from Florida. At 11 p.m. David got Luther discharged from the hospital. There was no point in staying and he wanted to be home. The sound of Jean's cries as she and Luther embraced was that of a loving, hurting, frightened mother and son. We tried to absorb what had just happened; what we had just heard. It was midnight and our house was as full as could be. I felt comforted. We were having a party! A party filled with people we love deeply and who loved us. It was one huge hug that I still feel today.

As the days unfolded, my brother-in-law, David, provided much needed comfort. He was able to answer any and all of our questions with knowledge, patience and great love. He spoke with the other physicians quicker and more capably than we ever could have. His gifts were put to use and brought us to the Mayo Clinic.

A Letter to the Congregation from Pastor Wright July 31, 2002

Dear Sisters & Brothers in Christ Jesus our Savior and Lord,

*I write this letter to all of you to inform you of the latest developments in my health status and treatment plans. The intent is to have every member of the congregation have a common and shared understanding of our situation. Please understand that all future dates are "planned" and subject to change. **A bit of history:** In mid-June I began to suffer a series of painful "attacks" felt throughout my chest, abdomen and back. The attacks would come during the night and then subside by daybreak. On July 1, I went to the emergency room and was initially treated for an apparent heart attack. After 12 hours of treatment and tests the doctors concluded that I had not had a heart attack, but was evidently suffering from gall bladder problems. I was discharged to the care of my primary physician with the expectation that I would soon undergo gall bladder surgery. However, just twenty-four hours later—on July 2—I suffered another one of the painful "attacks" and went back to the emergency room for medical intervention. Directing their attention to the previously* *diagnosed gall bladder problem, the doctors ordered some tests. After completing tests on July 3 the doctors concluded that there was an apparent malignant tumor "choking off" the biliary ducts that drain bile from the liver into the gall bladder and small intestine. A replaceable stent was inserted to drain the bile. A final test on July 4 confirmed their diagnosis. Further analysis led to this dismal prognosis: 1) This particular kind of malignant tumor ("cholangiocarcinoma") was resistant to radiation and chemotherapies, and 2) The position of the tumor led them to believe that it was inoperable. I was discharged from the hospital late in the evening of July 4.*

On Friday afternoon July 12 I was able to get a second opinion from one of the top surgeons at The Karmanos Cancer Institute in Detroit. He confirmed the diagnosis and the dismal prognosis. However he held out a single hope. He thought the Mayo Clinic in Rochester, MN had developed a clinical trial involving 'Liver Transplant with radiation and chemo therapies program' that had been successful in at least a few cases. He told me to contact Mayo immediately and investigate this single avenue of hope.

On Monday morning July 15 I made contact with Mayo Clinic. Results of the phone interview indicated that I appeared to fit the profile to justify traveling to Mayo for further evaluation. I was asked to report to the Mayo Clinic at 6:30 AM on Wednesday, July 17.

Sarah and I flew to Rochester, MN Tuesday afternoon July 16. The first phase/ "Initial Evaluation" began on July 17 and ended on July 26. On Friday afternoon we received the GOOD NEWS that the malignant tumor had apparently not metastasized and spread to any other part of the body. This GOOD NEWS was crucial, because if the cancer spreads beyond the tumor then I am immediately disqualified from the liver transplant program.

Because the tumor appears to be contained I get to move on to the second phase/ "Radiation and Chemo Therapies". The goal is to keep the tumor contained for as long as it takes for me to "qualify" for a liver transplant. It may take anywhere from 6-18 months to receive a liver transplant. The annual "economics" of liver transplantation comes to this bottom line: approximately 17,000 folks need a liver transplant each year; 5,000 will receive a transplant this year; 5,000 folks who need a transplant will die this year without ever receiving a transplant; and 7,000 folks on this year's "waiting list" will roll over to next year's waiting list.

Comments:

The first phase/ "Evaluation" concluded that aside from the golf ball-size malignant tumor encasing my biliary ducts and the liver artery and vein, I am apparently in excellent health for a 43-year-old male. The doctors feel that overall I am in great shape to begin the second phase/ "Chemo & Radiation Therapies"…

Celebrations:

It is an understatement to say that it has been an awful month for Sarah, Amy, Ben and me. It is even more of an understatement to testify that it has been an AWE-FULL month for the four of us. For our God is indeed an AWESOME GOD! Let me recount for you just a few of the AWE-FULL snapshots from our "Count

Our Many Blessing Photo-Album" for July 2002.

- *Church members prayers flooding our hearts by sunrise 7/02*
- *Church member & hospital nurse accompanying us through the tests of 7/2 & 7/3*
- *Church members visiting and praying with Sarah and me in the hospital*
- *Church members preparing meals for Amy and Ben and checking on them.*
- *My brothers David (Memphis) and Don (New Jersey) and their wives Cindy and Carol Ann walking into my hospital room on the morning of the 4th of July.*
- *The Bishop coming into the lounge just seconds after.*
- *Church members bringing me and my family Holy communion in the hospital on July 5.*
- *Church members cooking dozens and dozens and dozens of meals to feed the two dozen extended family members who came to our home from 7/5 to 7/14.*
- *Church members setting up their pop-up camper that slept 10 of our family members out under the willow tree in the parsonage lawn.*
- *Church members and relatives flooding our mailbox and hearts with dozens upon dozens upon dozens of cards of hope. (All of which I will take with me to Mayo on 8/11 to re-read throughout the good times and tough times ahead.)*
- *Brother David Wright M.D. giving the congregation a summary of the events of 7/2-7.5.*
- *King of Kings Music Ministers & Board of Trustee Members leading the congregation in "The Service*

of The Word for Healing" on Sunday evening July 7. Cancer survivors sharing with me their testimonies of healing.

- *Church members serving as liaisons to direct and link the ever-abundant help offered by the congregation to meet our needs.*
- *Church members sacrificially, generously, abundantly giving us financial gifts to cover our immediate and short-term needs: Airplane tickets, motel, food and miscellaneous expenses.*
- *Church members checking on my Mom and Ben while and Sarah and I were at Mayo from 7/16 – 7/27.*
- *Church members stepping forward to meet the challenge of "running the good ship King of kings" under the Captaincy of Christ while deck-hand Luther is in sick bay.*
- *Have I mentioned the Mayo Clinic? It deserves a "Count our many Blessings Album of its own! The staff at the Mayo Clinic make it a medical center worthy of its world-renowned reputation! The hospital-ity, the compassion, the excellence, the encouragement, the personalism of the staff is truly AWE-FULL!*

<u>In Closing</u>

We have been to the depths of medical despair—July 3-11---and God was faithful in His love for us in our depths of despair. His Light burned bright as the harvest moon in our darkness and the darkness did not overcome His own brilliant Light! Thank God for the Healing Service of July 7!!! I am the God that healeth thee!!!

We have been to the brink of medical hope---July 12...and God was faithful in His love for us as faint beams of medical hope brightened the dark sky. His Light burned bright as the same Easter Son-Rise that dismissed the darkness on Easter morn shined upon us! Shine, Jesus, Shine!!!

We now stand at the threshold of medical promise---July 26 & August 12 and beyond...And God is faithful in His love for us as a magnificent experimental treatment lights up our future with the Light of His Promises! O God our Help in ages past, our Hope for years to come!!!

And now we wait in faithfulness to the love of God in the obedience of the prophet Isaiah who testified:

Why do you dare say and speak, "My way is hid from the Lord, my life is disregarded by God"?

Have you not known? Have you not heard?

The Lord is the everlasting God, the Creator of the ends of the earth. He does not faint or grow weary, his understanding is unsearchable. He gives power to the faint, and to the one who has no might He increases their strength.

Even the young shall faint and be weary and fall exhausted:

BUT they who wait for the Lord shall renew their strength, they shall mount up with wings like eagles, they shall run and not be weary, they shall walk and not faint!" Isaiah 40: 27-30.

How 'bout joining me on this daily walk with Jesus?

Luther's e-mail to family and friends
August 24, 2002

Dear Family & Friends,

Hope all is well with each of you. Thought I'd give you a quick update on things with me at Mayo. Yesterday afternoon I received radiation treatment #20 out of 30. (Started treatments on 8/12 and will finish them on 8/30). Carried by the grace of God and love of all who are praying for me I am receiving maximum benefits with minimum side-effects. I've been able to walk a couple of miles each day, have been able to eat 3 squares and 3 snacks a day and thus maintain my weight. (My personal dietician on the Liver Transplant Team gave me this simple RX: More calories, more fat, more protein=eat anything I'm hungry for any time I want= one of the silver linings in the cloud).

Sarah, Ben and Amy flew into town on Wednesday 8/14 and then flew home on Monday 8/19. I felt good enough last Saturday to take the family to the Mall of America. I was able to get the last available motorized cart and thus jet around the LARGEST ENCLOSED MALL in the world and not get fatigued. We were there until closing. The kids were able to pick up some school clothes. Sarah and the kids were able to ride several of the amusement rides that are in the center of the mall.

On Monday, I was able to move into the Gift of Life Transplant House that is just 2 blocks from the Clinic. I have my own private bedroom and bath, and then share common cooking, TV, recreation, exercise and computer areas with the other 47 patients and their 47 caregivers. The credo of the House is this: Live Well – Love Much – Laugh Often. I call it the house of miracles---folks in either the pre-transplant, post-transplant, or follow-

up to transplant process for livers, kidneys, hearts, pancreas', stem cells and bone marrow. I am humbled by the faith and courage I see in my housemates and their care-givers.

My big brother Don flew into town last night and is staying with me as my care-giver through the end of treatments next Friday. He and I are driving a couple of hours north this afternoon to spend the night with a Pastor friend of mine back from my internship in Denver in '84-'85—Craig is the director of Luther Pointe Bible Camp in rural Wisconsin—so Don and I will get a change of scenery for 24 hours; we'll be back home to the Transplant house Sunday evening.

My oldest nephew Tim (big brother Dave's eldest son) is flying in on Wednesday 8/28 and will be with me through the end of treatment. He, Don and I will be three wild and crazy guys in the otherwise quiet, serene and conservative confines of Mayo-ville!

As plans stand today (plans that are always subject to change!) I'll fly home next Friday or Saturday and then be home until September 15. Sarah and I will fly back to Mayo on Sunday, and then on Monday the 16th I'll begin the continuous chemo that will be my daily bread for x days and months unto transplant. On Tuesday I'll be admitted to the hospital as an inpatient and undergo a 24-72 hour treatment whereby radium "seeds" will be implanted into the tumor. After the "seeds" are removed, either Wednesday or Thursday, I'll be discharged from the hospital on the chemo. They've asked me to stay in town until Saturday at which time we'll fly home. At that point I'll lay low for 10 days or so and then around 10/1 assess my health and energy and immune system status and trajectory and make some initial significant life decisions about my return to pastor King of Kings for the fall.

The Big Question is when I will go to transplant. God only knows. The doctors are understandably reluctant to try to answer what is truly an un-answerable question from a human point of view. The most they'll say it is could be up a year from now. So I will continue to seek to "trust only Jesus always" day-by-day living well, loving much and laughing often. My prayer is that this gift be yours too.

Big Question #2: Have you made the legally binding decision to become an organ donor? (And no I'm not blood thirsty for your liver). If not, I humbly ask you to begin to make the soul-conscious choice to address that decision as soon as possible. Yes I now have a cause to give myself to zealously! Seriously, I simply ask you to intentionally make a conscious decision. I have learned that the only binding contract for organ donors is to have it legally documented—I have also learned that the check this box spot on your driver's license is NOT legally binding. Another key thing is to let your nearest and dearest know your desire in the event the unthinkable happens before you get your decision in writing. Yesterday is history, tomorrow is a mystery, today is a gift that is why it is called "the present". I will now step off my soapbox.

I feel your prayers through the many and various ways God has been answering them---My gratitude journal expands by volumes each day. Thank you for your love for me and for Sarah and Amy and Ben--- Thank you for all the ways that each of you in your own special way has made that spiritual love and care for us absolutely real and material. You will never, ever know what strength your love has given me, has given us to walk this journey with our Lord. I thank God for you, truly I do.

I hope you have a great weekend. Give those most precious to you gifts from the heart today. Cherish the wonder of life as you "love the ones you're with"!

LOVE YA, Luther

Chapter 4

Jimmerz

"A friend loves at all times."
Proverbs 17:17

Luther Lee Wright
LLW
LUTH
FRIEND

Letter from Jim Stuef, close and dear friend
October, 2004

How do I start to tell my story about Luther's love
and friendship for me and my family? I guess the best
place to start is the beginning.

Luther started loving my family back before I knew him
at all, he was my future sister-in-law's (Dana's) pastor
at Truth and my brother (Mike) worked with Luther one
summer. He also was at my Mom's funeral and Mike
and Dana's wedding. Luther was friends with my high
school football coach and my best friend from high
school, both of whom I had not seen in years. I still had
not met this Luther guy and only knew him as: the guy
with the big beard.

My wife Greta and our family became members

at King of Kings in fall of 1995. Two months later the pastor announced his plans to take a new call. So, the course was set and plans were made to find Luther Lee Wright and unite him with his long lost brother Jimmerz from Hazeltucky and the Stuef family.

Once the call committee began its search we prayed to God for much guidance and several miracles, and he answered with Luther, Sarah, Amy, Bennyhana and Toby (let's not forget the most loved dog in the world) I figure Luther and his family were the miracles and the guidance would come later because how do you follow Hyperboy Luther and his crazy antics, Christian and otherwise. I will attempt to describe some of Luther's antics the best I can remember, so hold on to your ____, close your eyes, plug your ears and nose, this will be my view of One Hyperactive, Jesus Loving, Jesus Freak, Luther Wright!!!

I cannot place these events chronologically, so I will write them based on how they fall from my head and on how they impacted my life and my family's.

Our first run: Luther tried to kill me one late summer afternoon, the run from hell as I like to call it. We started the event just like any run starts out slow and conversational. That's where things get distorted because Luther did not slow his pace of running or talking for the rest of the event. I, however, had only been training at the rate of a normal human being prior to this run from hell, so I was out of breath and stamina at the two mile marker which was only half way. Luther noticed I was not doing so well. To make me feel better, he ran backward so I would not need to turn my head as he continued his sermon. Somewhere during this run Luther told me in layman terms what he thought about God's creation, "the black flies which attack him on runs." The end did not come soon enough for now I was on the insider list, that's the list that gives you the privilege to know Luther as a friend, not just your pastor. I was not sure at first if being on the insider list was a good thing, but Luther would prove to me that going on the run would be the best mistake of my life.

Our first Date: We had tried to get together for dinner for sometime and finally the moon and the stars and all the planets aligned and Luther and Sarah found time in their schedules to have a date. We know how busy pastors can be or do we? As we drove to the restaurant Luther and I in the front seats and Sarah and Greta in the back, we came around a bend in the road. There we saw an old woman who had fallen over in her wheel chair. Luther said, "stop the car," as he reached for his door handle at the speed of 50 mph. I had noticed the woman, but also the five other people who were already assisting her, so I continued at 50 mph. Luther insisted we go back. We did. I knew then what kind of person Luther was. He would stop just in case there was any remote chance that person might need him for something. He had time for others even if he was traveling at 50 mph. He put others first always, though there were five others standing around her, Luther and I picked her up and made sure she was going to be okay. She may still be lying there if Luther had not insisted we help. Oh yeah, dinner was great and I shared the black fly story with Sarah and Greta which then put Greta on the "insider list" as well. Sorry Greta.

Our first slumber party: Luther had been dealing with

some very difficult politics at our church and he needed a break. So we made plans to camp on Lake Huron for the night (90 miles north of Detroit). We packed our bags, kissed our wives good-bye and were off, just the two of us. I wish our wives had come along. Upon our arrival as we paid the park fee to the ranger he asked if we would be having any visitors (female visitors), as he winked at us as we drove into the state park. We really wished our wives were with us. The entire camp was filled with couples. That should have put us at ease, though it only made things worse, but quite humorous. We set up camp near the water, went for a kayak ride and a swim. Seems harmless enough, right? As dinnertime rolled around we could feel the eyes around us beginning to stare. I'm sure it was just our imagination. Still it was quite humorous. The night air was filled with the sound of "gee I wish our wives were here." Oh yeah, and much laughter. When we woke the next morning, Luther was on his side of the trailer and I was on mine, though we seemed much closer.

Luther believed that being a Christian was a blast. Joy filled to say the least. He did not want people to wonder what was wrong with him. He wanted them to know what he was high on, Jesus Christ!!! And God's people said Amen, and again Amen and one more time, Amen (Thanks Rudy). I heard a preacher on TV last night say, "don't let this world steal your joy." Jesus has won for us joy everlasting. Luther never allowed this world to tame his burning love for his Lord Jesus. Luther was able to meet God's people where they were. He was able to relate to all people in all walks of life. Luther was truly a gift from God to us that were blessed to know him.

Our first Halloween: Luther would almost always signal his arrival to our house with blaring music, horns blowing and tires squealing. This would let our children know it was time to run and hide, especially when they were young. During that first Halloween Lydia and Rachel were in bed when the Wrights stopped in, probably sleeping and dreaming of ghost and goblins as would be expected on Halloween eve. Luther would not wake sleeping children, or at least I would not think he would. Remember this is our first Halloween so we were still getting to know the man with the big beard. Lydia and Rachel were 6 and 4 years old and sleeping when Luther and Sarah arrived. As big as Luther's beard could have ever been, his voice was bigger, or should I say HIS SCREAM was louder. The car drove up the drive and was loud enough for Greta and me to know that the Wrights were here and the girls must have heard something for they stirred. The door opened and Luther and Sarah walked in and Luther was being quite loud. Surprised? I didn't think so!! The girls were now awake. They came to the stairs and said hello in a shy sort of fearful way. After a few questions from Luther about the big haul of candy, the girls headed back to bed. Luther and Sarah stayed for about a half hour just talking in the kitchen and then it was time to leave. A short nice visit between friends and all was well. Out the door they went. Not so fast, you say. Luther decided to sneak up the stairs to say good night to two unsuspecting girls. He really did not warn any of us, the girls included, of what he was going to do. All at once Luther let out the most blood curdling scream. Our hearts jumped into our throats, our eyes teared up and the girls screamed just as loud in response. Lydia and Rachel now know the man with the big beard was really the world's biggest crack head and they were in tears, Greta was ready to strangle the man. This is my story and I remember it that way, though I could be mixing up other times Luther tried to scare us to death.

My first football war with Luther: Woody Hayes could not match Luther's enthusiasm for college football, in particular Ohio State and Florida State. This was a year when I thought I had Luther where I wanted him. Cooper was still the OSU coach. Having said this, the Buckeyes would eventually lose to the Michigan Wolverines, but this is not the memory I have. It was a play between University of Michigan and Michigan State University that lives on in my mind. The play cost Michigan a shot at the National Title game. Whatever the play was, it was obvious the incorrect call was made against the beloved Wolverines. I remember the call; the time-keeper cheated and gave the Spartans an extra play when the clock should have run out. Luther and Sarah had us over for something and Luther pops in a tape of the game. He recorded the event so he could tease me over and over and in slow motion even. He was laughing so hard and I, of course, found no humor in this little prank. That was only the beginning of our love affair with sports and things Luther thought were sports.

A big time wrestling match: Luther believed that all people loved or should love Wrestle mania. I grew up in a community where real wrestling started at the age of 4 and continued forever. I have never, to this day, watched a Big time wrestling match in its entirety. This only encouraged Luther to try and win me over to the fake side. He loved a challenge. He would call me on the phone at all hours of the night and tell me, in a wild voice, turn the TV to channel whatever so I could see some wrestling star do some unbelievable stunt. Most time I would humor him and do as he commanded, and I would always laugh at his play by play commentary. Luther finally saw the light when a wrestler from OSU won the NCAA championship. A funny thing happened after that though. This guy from OSU started writing me letters and wanted to kick my butt in a wrestling match, for some unknown reason! I really think it was Luther in disguise writing these letters. Do ya think?!!

The Sleepy Bear camping trip: Luther and I left out at 2:00 a.m. for the Platt River National Campground on Lake Michigan, drove four hours, only to stand in line with 30 other people for a possible 10 openings on the 4th of July weekend. We thought for sure we would be near the front of the line if there was to be a line at all. We were 25th in that line. Not quite the front. So for plan "B" we had driven past a place called the Sleepy Bear Campground with a vacancy sign out front. We made it there and got the last campsite for the long weekend. This would prove to be a fantastic campground, just about perfect. Our wives and families showed up later that morning along with two of Ben's friends, Donnie and Scott. We enjoyed camping and all the fun you could possibly fit into a holiday weekend that summer. We spent a long time at the Sleeping Bear Dunes National Lakeshore hiking and swimming. This was most likely the best camping trip ever. We laughed a lot, we ate the best food and we loved every minute we spent together.

Luther Gandhi: In the last fall of Luther's life our families traveled to an away high school football game. The game was against the state's best football team in the last 30 years. This school is where I presently teach, though at the time I worked at another high school across town. When we arrived the away bleachers were filled and with Luther very weak, we chose to sit on the home side which as it turned out was our first mistake. We felt very confident that our team was going to beat this power house and this made me feel a bit cocky (second BIG mistake). We sat down and our wives left to use the restroom that left us alone with the enemy crowd of several thousand, BIG mistake #3. I opened the team program to the centerfold of the 15 time Michigan High School Football State Champions team photo. We weren't impressed, though something inside must have been because I started making negative comments in a rather loud voice to show how unimpressed I really was. These comments were overheard by a few fans that really did not appreciate my sense of humor or the tone in my voice. As a matter of fact, they became quite angry and began to swear at Luther and me. I normally would have not said two words back to these gentlemen, but this was one of those times (did I mention I was feeling a little cocky) so I spoke back to these fellows. I responded to the attack in the only way you could when you are with your sick friend and pastor. I cursed them up one side and down the other. BIG mistake #4. Now I've started something that only God could get us out of alive.

Remember I'm counting on Luther to get my back,

all 125lbs of his cancer filled body, BIG MISTAKE #..................As God says, he will always leave a window open if you close the door in your own face. Well this window turned out to be a former student who was sitting near by. He recognized me as the varsity wrestling coach at the across town rival. He spoke and called me by name and this somehow stopped the mob for a moment. I looked down at Luther, for I was standing in the "do you want a piece of me" position ready to fight. Luther said "can't we just get along?" which was starting to make a lot of sense right about then. So I did some quick talking and the fight was avoided. God not only saved us but I learned that being loud and cocky is really a bad idea especially in the enemy's camp with half your troop wounded (Luther, Liver Cancer, Duh Stupid!!!). God knows how to bring home a message so you don't forget. Our great quarterback went down for the season the third play of the game and we lost 21-7.

I miss Luther because life with him was always an adventure. You always knew to expect laughter and excitement. I have many other stories that pass through my mind and every day I thank God for the time we had together. His life in Jesus still blesses us each day. Sometimes we don't even realize it and sometimes we see it as plain as day. I'll share one last story and this goes with that saying "save the best for last".

Greta and I have three wonderful children. They all loved Luther and he loved them more than we know. He called them to his death bed to speak to each of them individually, to say, see you in Heaven on your Easter. These words to our children were the last coherent words that he spoke to our family. His love for our girls *will impact their lives forever. He showed the Savior's love to the end, caring for others, not for himself, right to the grave. God used Luther to change our lives to help us better understand Trusting Only Jesus Always.*

I don't know how to end this so I won't, because it doesn't end. Luther still impacts us. As an example, our daughter Lydia was completing a packet of information to prepare for her confirmation. A question in the packet (which was prepared by Luther for past confirmation years) was "Who is the most influential person in your life? Lydia's response was, you guessed it, Luther Lee Wright. And God's people say Amen, Amen, and one more time Amen!!!!

Chapter 5

The Wilderness

"I am about to do a new thing; now it springs forth, do you not perceive it?
I will make a way in the wilderness and rivers in the desert." Isaiah 43:19

Luther notes in his devotional on June 4, 2003 "My Exodus from hospital." He trusted God's work in the darkness/wilderness as if it were the light of day.

I found myself struggling with some difficult questions: what is God's purpose in this wilderness? Will I trust God to lead me through this? I began reading from Luther's Bible from Isaiah 43: 18-21…'I will make a way in the wilderness'…All of us in this life here on earth will pass through a wilderness or two where we have to look to see where God is taking us. Looking back to that day in our driveway, Luther, our friend, Gary and myself were having a discussion on God's provisions in the wilderness when God answered our questions. As we were talking, Luther asked us, "Would God provide a table in the wilderness?" To our amazement a delivery truck pulled into our driveway. Soon the man was walking up to us with a beautiful and HUGE basketful of wonderful pastries from a family at church. The three of us looked at each other and began laughing loudly at God's provision for us in this wilderness of cancer. The answer was clear, God says, "Yes, I can provide a table in the wilderness." Do I trust God in this, with this, through this? Yes, I most certainly do. People have often wondered why God doesn't show himself like he did 'back then.' I have seen God show himself to me each and every day in this wilderness and I am continually reminded that for today God's grace is sufficient in any and all my circumstances. Luther wrote in his Bible, June 23, 2004, "Come and sit and listen and laugh with me at all the Lord has done, is now doing and has promised to do for me." We could see that God continued to work and fight for us in this cancer wilderness.

From Luther to George, our friend from the Mayo Clinic with cholangiocarcinoma
September 14, 2002

Dear George,

Glad that you are doing well---all things considered! I imagine that the seven weeks in Mayo-ville was difficult in many ways. I know that after the two weeks of being there for evaluation in July, it was great to be able to come home for a couple of weeks, and the same holds true after Phase 1 of treatment, it was great to get home for a couple of weeks before upcoming Phase two. From a spiritual standpoint, I found being in Mayo-ville in general, and the Transplant House in particular, a two-sided coin type of experience: There is the tremendous encouragement that comes from seeing all the "walking miracles". At the same time, there is a tremendous strain from seeing the pain and suffering.

Since I've been home I've been studying and re-reading the books of Exodus, Numbers, Deuteronomy and Joshua: The Story of God's deliverance of the Israelites from Egypt, their 40 year journey through the wilderness, and their entry into the Promised Land.

I have particularly been able to identify with it on a personal basis in this way: "Egypt" represents for me my life before my fateful diagnosis on Wednesday, 7/3. It is a life that I will never be able to return to..."The Exodus" represents my life on the date of Thursday 7/25---the date Dr. Gores welcomed me as a patient in the Liver Transplant Treatment Program..."The Wilderness Journey" represents my life from that day forward up through the transplant next year..."The Promised Land" represents my life after transplant.

For the ancient Israelites, the journey from Egypt to the Promised Land involved the round about way of the wilderness. In the wilderness God's exodus act of deliverance and God's promise of the best future was to be met with trust & gratitude + obedience = faith in God. But instead of the wilderness period being a time where their faith was to shine, their wilderness journey became primarily a period of unbelief + ingratitude + rebellion = No faith in God. Again and again the people complained against God, questioning both His presence/absence in their midst AND His faithfulness/lack of faithfulness to deliver them to the Promised Land.

AND YET---this is the Gospel of the Old Testament---the story of Exodus-Wilderness-Entry in the Promised Land is carried through by the love and faithfulness *of God because despite the people's blindness and rebellion, our God of unconditional <u>love, grace and mercy</u> remained faithful to every single one of His promises: "Not one of all the good promises that the Lord had made the house of Israel failed; all came to pass": <u>Joshua 21:4.</u>*

In the wilderness the people of God were being discipled so that they might know their utter dependence upon the God who freed them from their slavery in Egypt and thus be strengthened for the new challenges of a new life in the new land, the Promised Land.

Psalm 78: 1-25 is a wonderful psalm that ties together the essential themes and lessons from this period. Verse 19 reduces the faith struggle of the wilderness period to a single question: "Can God spread a table for us in the wilderness?"

This is the fundamental faith question I've had to struggle with as I've looked ahead to and through the radiation and chemo therapies and the indeterminate number of months on the "waiting list"...At first I envisioned "the wait" as something to truly suffer through, day by day, week by week, month by month,---hoping hoping, hoping that I make it to transplant before the cancer spreads...Envisioned this way, I didn't see that there was much good to come out of the "waiting period"—if anything I saw it as cruel time both for me in going through the pre-transplant therapies and tests, and for my dear family having to witness my slow demise.

After my re-reading of Exodus-Numbers,

Deuteronomy and Joshua + The 4 Gospels I've now been able to re-frame the "waiting period" as "a wilderness" in which God does indeed spread a feast table (Psalm 78:19) for me and my family---and thus this time of waiting is not a cruel time, a time to merely suffer through---but it is a time when the grandest of gifts---being discipled into complete and utter dependence upon God as my everything and my all in all---is being served up for me on a daily basis--- This experience of being so discipled is the absolutely essential preparation I need for the new challenges of the new life after Transplant---And as I re-frame things through this lens of faith, I can trust that the precise chronological length of my wait has everything to do with length of time God sees as necessary for my "faith schooling" and little if anything to do with things like the numbers of livers available, my "score" on the liver transplant rating system, etc.

Transplant is truly a matter of God's will and God's timing...in this I find the peace that passes all understanding...I find this peace confirmed in the spiritual transplant I am undergoing day by day: "A new heart I will give you, and a new spirit I will put within you; and I will remove from your body the heart of stone and give you a heart of flesh. I will put my spirit within you." Ezekiel 36:26

That's where I am today, in this leg of the wilderness journey...Asking again that this day, this hour, this moment that God's all-sufficient grace be All that God desired it be for me.

You and Carla and your family remain in our

prayers…May God lead you in the special path He has for you so that you may be "weller than well" each day in this journey of faith, hope and love…

God Bless You! Your brother in Christ, Luther

From Luther
November 26, 2002

Dear Family & Friends,

Happy Thanksgiving Eve! I hope that gratitude will be the main course of your feast tomorrow. Barbara Johnson points out: "Something to be thankful for is that you're here to be thankful."

I just want to drop you a short update on the events of yesterday so that you can hear it from the "horse's mouth."

As you know, the Mayo Clinic projects (based on the rules and regulations of organ distribution) that I will not receive a liver transplant until sometime next fall. However, in the event that a person designates their cadaver liver to me, the liver transplant could happen immediately.

Such was the case yesterday. From noon to 6 p.m. was one of the most emotional stretches in my (and count Sarah, Amy & Ben in on this too) entire life.

A local man's wife and family had designated me to be the recipient of his liver. The man suffered a severe heart attack on Sunday morning. It took 10 tries (over a 67 minute period) with the electric heart paddle to revive him; unfortunately by that point he had suffered major brain damage. By Monday evening doctors informed the man's wife that he was brain dead. One of the man's brothers was unable to fly into town until late Tuesday afternoon; the family hoped and prayed that the man would remain alive until his brother could pay his last respects.

At about noon on yesterday the man's family, knowing my plight, decided to take the necessary steps to donate his liver to me. We found out that our blood types matched, and that the size of his liver was a proper "fit" for me. At this point the organ donor officials from the hospital contacted my Liver Transplant Team surgeons at Mayo for a consultation; the regional and national organ donor board officials were also in on the conversation. After a thorough review of my case and a thorough analysis of the offered liver, my surgeons at Mayo deliberated for several hours (in the meantime we had arranged with "Angel Flights" to fly us out at 10 p.m. that night) and then made the decision to decline the offered liver.

We got the call from Mayo while sitting in the waiting room of my oncologists, Dr. Amnuay Singhowkowinta, MD and Dr. Sobilo, MD (yesterday also happened to be my monthly check-up and dispensing of the pills for my third cycle of chemo which started this morning).It was a crushing blow; much as we had braced ourselves for things not working out, in six hours our hopes had grown full bloom, especially after we found out that the liver was a "match," and that an "Angel Flight" had been arranged against long odds given the holiday week.

The nurse coordinator of the Liver Transplant Team

explained the decision to me thusly: 1) The doctors felt that given the condition of the offered liver was in less than optimal condition due to the fact that it took 10 tries over the course of 67 minutes to revive the man, and 2) given that my death is not imminent, and 3) given the fact that there is a substantial risk of death in the liver transplant surgery, the doctors felt it best not to take such a risk at this time with a less than optimal liver.

While I must submit to my surgeons' decisions, I do wrangle with reason #2: The "race" that I'm running is to get to transplant before the cancer spreads; and it stands to reason that my best chance to win this "race" is to do the transplant sooner rather than later, better yesterday or today, than tomorrow.

Several positives came out of yesterday: Blessing #1) I believe that the family was going to go ahead and donate as many organs and tissues as possible, it seemed likely that there would be someone who would receive his "less than optimal liver", so that is indeed good news amid the terrible tragedy the family was experiencing, up to 67 people can benefit from one donor. Blessing #2): The possibility of yesterday has got me to thinking about taking another course than that of just sitting back and waiting for the year to pass to receive a liver through the standard organ procurement and distribution process which is definitely skewed against my particular circumstance, my "race" to get to transplant before the cancer spreads and thus disqualifies me from transplant. Perhaps I need to get the word out that a person can designate a liver for me, provided of course that it is an appropriate "match" in the eyes of my transplant surgeons. Quite frankly, I'm still a bit numb from yesterday's roller coaster, and I'm not so sure how I feel about "soliciting" for a liver amid the competitive and uneven field of "play" among the 17,000 or so folks who are as desperate for a liver as I am; on the flip side, it seems that whatever little/ much I can do to uplift the need and the "miracles" of organ donation more than justifies whatever I may do to "solicit" for my own life, AND IT'S HERE THAT I'M ASKING FOR YOUR PRAYERS THAT GOD GIVE ME WISDOM & COUNSEL ON HOW TO PROCEED WITH "ALL OF THIS", and Blessing #3): The results of yesterday's oncology appointment are great. I'm thriving under the oral chemotherapy protocol, my blood work all falls within the normal range for a non-cancer, no chemo person! Praise God!

Soooo, that's what new from my neck of the woods.

I want you to know that I thank God for your love, friendship & prayers. I can't imagine what it would be like to be going through this without your one-of-a-kind show of support. I pray that amid your tests and trails you will be equally blessed with such love, friendship, prayers and support.

"O give thanks to the Lord, for He is good; for His steadfast love endures forever." Psalm 107:1

"Rejoice in the Lord always, again I say rejoice!" Philippians 4:4

"In everything give thanks." I Thessalonians 5:18

"To be grateful is to recognize the love of God in everything He has given us, and He has given us

everything." Thomas Merton

"Gratitude. More aware of what you have than what you don't. Recognizing the treasure in the simple, a child's hug, fertile soil, a golden sunset. Relishing in the comfort of the common, a warm bed, a hot meal, a clean shirt." Max Lucado

HAPPY THANKSGIVING! All our love, Luther, Sarah, Amy & Ben

Chapter 6

Rising Above

"I will tell of the LORD's unfailing love.
I will praise the LORD for all he has done.
I will rejoice in his great goodness to Israel,
which he has granted according to his mercy and love."
Isaiah 63:7

Luther often spoke about God playing the "Lazarus card" for him. There were many times when the nights had no end and the excruciating agony lasted for hours with no relief. He would get in and out of bed pacing throughout the house, unable to get comfortable. Luther had already been wearing pain patches. We would then add a combination of pills, still no relief. Then liquid morphine: STILL no relief. As a last resort I would give him an injection of morphine. It was a nightmare. The first time I did it, I felt confident, gave him the injection and then cried. Emotionally this was a torturous process for me because it inflicted added pain along with the fear of accidental overdose. We would eventually fall asleep and I would awaken with a start wondering, "Is he still breathing?" Finally, when the new morning dawned, he would look at me with that smile and say, "Well Lazarus is alive again…" What a relief it was to hear Luther's sense of humor and faith and to know we had made it through another night.

Even after tough episodes, Luther wasted no time

ministering to others, remaining faithful and hopeful trusting only Jesus always no matter what the situation. He had a gift of rising above his own circumstances, taking the focus from himself and turning it to whomever he was talking to.

Jesus heard of Lazarus' sickness and then waited four more days to go there. Keep in mind that Jesus' actions were/are never hurried. God's timing is never late but always right on time. Everything He did or does or said was done to show God's glory. Always. Even through Luther's illness God's Glory was shown. (And let me say, His glory did shine.) His love did and does abound. When Luther was first diagnosed a dear friend from church came to visit. As he hugged Luther, crying, she said, "I don't know why this is happening. I guess God wants to show us a miracle." I thought about that many times. Even though the miracle we wanted of a cure and health was not God's miracle, many more miracles occurred. Luther took to calling me Mrs. Lazarus. I loved being called Mrs. Lazarus. In his Bible at Isaiah 63:7 he wrote 'Mr. & Mrs. Lazarus "God, our Helper, there is nothing too hard, too wonderful, too amazing, too beautiful for the God of love to do for him who loves us." "Come & sit & listen & laugh with me at all the Lord God has done, is now doing and has promised he will do for me!" I believe he was, had been, seeing Jesus. His faith was tremendous even as his body got sicker and weaker. Yes, he saw Jesus. He showed me what he saw and believed with his whole heart, mind, soul and spirit.

From Luther to Rich and Pauline, friends.
Feb. 13, 2002.

Dear Rich-n-Pauline,

I'm reading a book titled, <u>Touch The Top Of The World</u> by Erik Weihenmayer, the blind mountain climber who has reached the seven highest summits in the world. In the Introduction he talks about climbing Long's Peak in the month of January as a preparatory climb for Mt. McKinley. He calls Long's Peak "a rough fourteener", a higher more difficult peak, one often considered the most grueling in Colorado! Dude, we climbed it together 18 years ago! I feel better reading his estimation of our accomplishment because I have always told people that climbing Long's Peak was the single most difficult physical feat I've completed. I'll never forget standing on top of the world with you and snapping pictures on the summit plate.

So I got to thinking...How 'bout after our respective recoveries are complete ...say in 2005 (my estimated recovery date...I'm logging your back recovery for '03!) or so, you, me and our boys (and wives and girls if they want) climb Long's Peak. I'll be 47 and I think that'll make you about 51. Whadda you think?

They have a thing called the "Transplant Games" that occur every four years. I'm hoping one day to participate in that too.

I'd like to share with you a spiritual thought that helps me along each day: I call it "The Lazarus Card". You are no doubt familiar with the two Lazarus's in the New Testament: John 11 – Jesus' dear friend who he resurrected from the dead (which just so happened to be the last straw for those who sought to kill him) & Luke 16- Jesus' parable about the rich man and the poor man named Lazarus. Well the name Lazarus means "God helps/ God is my Help". In both of these Bible stories we have the clear testimony that man's/women's only hope is to place our trust in the help of God.

Well with that in my mind and spirit, a few months back, in one particular circumstance of desperation I prayed to God-and-simultaneously said to Sarah, "I need God to pull off a Lazarus miracle for me. Well "God who is my Help" did exactly that.

And ever since then, whenever I/we find ourselves in dire straits, I'll pray aloud, "God, I need you to pull off another Lazarus miracle for me." And because He is the Faithful One, He has answered me/us each time with His Help.

It's gotten to the point that each time I/we pray this prayer we begin rejoicing-smiling-laughing. Remember how in Genesis 18 Sarah's laugher at God when she was told that at the age of 91 she would conceive and bear a son to Abraham and then how The Lord Himself asked: "Is anything too hard, too wonderful for Me to accomplish?!" and then how in Genesis 21 the child was named "Isaac" which means "God has made laughter for me" in anticipation born of absolute faith-trust-belief that God will answer us with His Help, and that His Help will be sufficient for the circumstance at hand.

So now I tell folks that God playing the "Lazarus-card" for me is the Joker Card of my faith. I'm thinking that this is exactly what Paul discovered and then wrote about in Philippians 4 when he says, "Rejoice in the

Lord always; again I will say rejoice. The Lord is at hand. Have no anxiety about anything, but in everything by prayer and with thanksgiving (for past, present and future Lazarus-cards He has played/plays/will play on your behalf!) let your requests be made known to God. And the peace of God (isn't the joy of laughter the most wonderful "peace" a soul can enjoy?!), which passes all understanding, will keep your hearts and your minds in Christ Jesus. I can do all things in him who strengthens me. My God will supply every need of yours according to his riches in glory in Christ Jesus".

My prayer for y'all today is that God will play His Lazarus card for your circumstances. And I pray that even now, in celebration of the fact that He will be Your Help, you can laugh-smile, rejoice at the Joker Card of our faith, for Our Resurrection God always gets the last laugh & the final say over the devil, death, evil & sin in all our circumstances! Ah yes, Easter tells us that the devil at his worst is no match for God at His Best!!!

May God's Help for you be the best answer to all your prayers, this day and all days!

Love Ya, Luther

Personal Letter
December 23, 2004

From: Gregory J. Gores, M.D.
Medical Director of Liver Transplantation
Reuben R. Eisenberg Professor of Medicine Mayo Clinic

Dear Mrs. Wright:

I am writing somewhat belatedly in regard to your request. You asked me to write a few thoughts and words regarding Luther and his journey from my vantage point.

"Luther was a very endearing patient, one which I shall always remember. He approached his illness with courage and equanimity. Despite obvious disappointment and lack of definitive therapeutic options, he remained positive and realistic about his illness. I always felt that he was caught in the middle between basic human survival instincts and his religious training and background which focuses on the afterlife. I was also always struck by his positive approach to both. Most importantly, Luther sent me a book entitled "The Five People You Meet in Heaven" by Mitch Albom. Despite the fact that he sent me this book late in his illness, he remained upbeat and positive. This book is very important to me and has a very important place in my office. It sits on the ledge where I see it constantly to remind me of Luther and all that embodies. In particular, it reminds me of our humanity, the obvious failure of our current medical therapeutic armamentarium, and our need to do more. So Luther is there to constantly remind me of all this on a daily basis."

I hope you find the above helpful. I am sure that you miss Luther dearly. I know this has been a struggle for you, Amy and Ben, and you certainly have our condolences and our emotional and spiritual support.

Sincerely yours, Gregory J. Gores, MD

Chapter 7

Be Still

"God is our refuge and strength, always ready to help in times of trouble. Be still and know that I am God."
Psalm 46:1,10

While Luther was sick, I had a lot of anxiety. It was such an emotional roller coaster everyday. It was hard to be still. But when I was still I would feel such peace. The quiet was and is soothing to my soul.

Traveling to the Mayo clinic from Michigan became a continued part of our lives. We were faced with many new decisions with each visit. The unpredictability of life and learning to live life moment to moment, not knowing how long we would be away from home, and knowing the time clock was ticking away. The new course of attack presented to us was a Living Donor Liver Transplant (LDLT). The decision process regarding the LDLT was a difficult one. The one question Luther wrestled with the most was "If the donor, whoever it may be, were to become quite ill or die because of the transplant, could I live with that, as I grew stronger?"

From Luther
June 25, 2003

My Beloved Friends,

I pray that this letter finds you in good health and high spirits this summer season.

On June 18 & 19 Sarah and I were at the Mayo clinic for a round of tests. On June 18 I underwent blood work and a full abdominal CAT scan to assess the condition of my tumor. On June 19 we met with my transplant doctor, Dr. Greg Gores (who is also the Director of the Liver Transplant Program) to go over the test results.

The results indicate four things:

1. *The tumor has grown in size (the first change since diagnosis 7/3/02; my last CAT scan at Mayo was March '03)*
2. *Currently the cancer remains localized within the tumor.*
3. *The cancer cell activity within the tumor is aggressive; measured at 10-fold what it was in March '03.*
4. *The cancer will now continue to advance and is poised to spread beyond the tumor within the summer.*

The "original plan", the only plan, (confirmed most recently in March) was for Mayo to file a special appeal to the national organ distribution authority by late summer to advance me up the waiting list. Should the special appeal be granted, the hope was to have the transplant within six months of the appeal decision (early '04).

Dr. Gores told us that the June 18 results have the following immediate consequences for my life:

1. *The "original plan", the only plan, must be abandoned because the Liver Transplant Team has concluded that the cancer will spread long before I'd ever get to transplant via the special appeal route. My place on the national waiting list suggests a nine to twelve months waiting period for transplant time-frame rather than the previously hoped for six-month waiting period time-frame. Dire as my circumstances now are, they will not justify leap-frogging me over other persons on the list whose circumstances are equally dire for them. That's the bottom line of having 17,000 people on the waiting list with a projection of 5,000 cadaver donations in 2003.*

2. *Plan B has been conceived by the Liver Transplant Team and presented to me per this proposal: Living Donor Liver Transplant*

As you may recall, in July 2002 when we inquired about this possibility of a living donor liver transplant (LDLT), Dr. Gores informed us that a LDLT was not possible for patients with cholangiocarcinoma and that the only option was a cadaver transplant.

When Dr. Gores presented Plan B to us on July 19, 2003 he explained that three years ago Mayo has experimented with LDLT for four cholango patients. The results were ultimately fatal for the four patients and so Mayo declared a moratorium on LDLT for cholangio. Mayo has continued to do LDLT for a limited number of patients with other non-cancerous liver diseases with much success, a total of 13 over the three years.

This past winter ('02-'03) Mayo began to consider lifting the moratorium on LDLT for cholangio patients due to advances in the field of LDLT research and surgery. Mid-spring of this year the moratorium was lifted. LDLT was adopted as an experimental "Plan B option" for cholangio patients who had run out of options in just the dire straits I now find myself in – immediately close to cancer spreading and yet too far down on the waiting list to hope for a cadaver transplant.

Dr. Gores believes that as a cholangio patient I have some positive factors in my favor as the first LDLT in this new era of medicine in Mayo's Liver Transplant Program: my age, my overall health, my overall fitness, and my stable body weight.

Dr. Gores stressed that an LDLT is much more complicated surgery than a cadaver transplant and that there would be additional and more significant "bumps in the road for me" post-surgery.

In the event I consent to Plan B (more on that in the next paragraph), Dr. Gores would like to have me undergo the required exploratory surgery (where they "eyeball" my internal organs to check for the presence of cancer not detected through the non-invasive CAT scan) within the next 30 days. Provided the results of the exploratory surgery show that the cancer has not spread beyond the tumor site AND provided that a viable living donor liver transplant candidate has been identified by that point, they would like to give me a couple of weeks to recover before the LDLT. This projects out to the LDLT happening within the next 45-60 days.

Now about the matter of my consent ...a matter of first things first ...to state the obvious: In order for me to have the chance to gain life from the LDLT I require someone else who is in otherwise fine health to, at the very most self-lessly, sacrificially risk their life or, at the very least, the quality of their life (short term and perhaps long term) and for them to risk (at the very most) the end of or (at the very least) the quality of their precious relationships with their loved ones. AND in order for them to risk their life I require their loved ones to self-lessly, sacrificially risk (at the very most) the end or (at the very least) the quality of their precious relationship with the beloved donor ...all so my life and my relationships with my loves ones can continue ...a grave decision indeed ...first things first ...

Dr. Gores has asked me to reach a decision regarding the proposed Plan B within the week. And so we are now seeking God's will and direction for my decision. And I am humbly requesting that you who have faithfully kept us in your prayers now keep me and Sarah, Amy and Ben in your prayers with this particular focus, that our hearts and minds and wills be receptive to God's will and direction made plain in this circumstance.

At Christmas my dear friend Jim Eckert, our friendship dates back to our days as classmates at Trinity Lutheran Seminary '82—'86 hand delivered a Christmas present to me all the way from Cleveland. The gift was a copy of an annual-daily devotional reading called the <u>Streams in the Desert</u> by a woman named L.B. Cowman, and edited by James Reimann. It has been a treasured resource in my ongoing conversation with God that I have turned to daily since January 1.

I'd like to close this letter with an excerpt from the devotional from June 20, 2003:

Devotional Verse from the Old Testament
Thus says the Lord, "Whether you turn to the right or to

the left, your ears will hear my voice behind you, saying, 'This is the right way; walk in it" Isaiah 30:21

Devotion (S) Isaiah 30:15-21

When we have doubts or are facing difficulties, when others suggest courses of action that are conflicting, when caution dictates one approach but faith another, we should be still. We should quiet each intruding person, calm ourselves in the sacred stillness of God's presence, study His Word for guidance, and with true devotion focus our attention on Him. We should lift our nature into the pure light radiating from His face, having an eagerness to know only what God our Lord will determine for us. Soon He will reveal by His secret counsel a distinct and unmistakable sense of His direction…

Are you uncertain about which direction you should go? Take your question to God and receive His guidance. You must get alone with Him, where the lights and the darkness of this world cannot interfere and where the opinions of others cannot reach you. You must also have the courage to wait in silent expectation, even when everyone around you is insisting on an immediate decision or action.

If you will do these things, the will of God will become clear to you. And you will have a deeper experience of who He is, having more insight into His nature and being, and more intimacy with His heart of love. All this will be your unsurpassed gift.

Devotional Verse
"Stand Still," my soul, for so Your Lord commands:
E'en when your way seems blocked, leave it in His
wise hands:
His arm is mighty to divide the wave.

"Stand still", my soul, "stand still" and you will see
How God can work the "impossible" for thee,
For with a great deliverance He does save.

Be not impatient, but in stillness stand,
Even when surrounded on every hand,
In ways your spirit does not comprehend.
God cannot clear your way till you are still,
That He may work in you His blessed will,
And all your heart and will to Him do bend.

"BE STILL", my soul, for just when you are still,
Can God reveal Himself to you; until
Through you His love and light and life can
freely flow:
In stillness God can work through you and reach
The souls around you. He then through you can teach
His lessons, and His power in weakness show.

"BE STILL" – a deeper step in faith and rest.
"Be still and know" your Father does know best
The way to lead His child to that fair land,
A "summer" land, where quiet waters flow;
Where longing souls are satisfied, and "know
Their God,"
And praise for all that He has planned.

Streams in the Desert

Thank you for your unceasing unconditional love for me and Sarah, Amy and Ben these twelve months. Thank you for your love for us each and every day.

With your love and God's answers to your prayers for us we have truly been blessed and now will be able to "bear and endure all things" by the all-sufficient grace of God' by believing that with The True God revealed to us in the life and ministry and sacrifice and resurrection and ascension and Second Coming of Jesus, all things are possible, by knowing that all things work together for good for those who love God, and therefore hoping only in our God-of-Boundless-Hope ...who by the power at work within us is able to do far more abundantly than all we can ask or imagine filling us with all joy and peace and strength in believing so that we may continue to abound in faith, hope and love by the power of His Holy Spirit.

God Bless Us, Everyone!

Love, Luther

TRUSTING ONLY JESUS ALWAYS

From Luther
July 2, 2003

To: My Beloved Family and Friends

Thank you for your unceasing prayers on our behalf. Our faith, hope and love have truly been uplifted these past days by your love.

After much conversation with God I have decided to step onto the Living Donor Liver Transplant (LDLT) treatment pathway at the Mayo Clinic. I do so with the deepest faith in Jesus and his promise first pronounced to St. Paul in 55AD; "My grace is sufficient for you, for my power is made perfect in your weakness."

My decision was made in this precise and amazingly peace-full surrender: "Gracious Father, in this situation this is what I have discerned to be what it is to trust only Jesus always. I trustfully and joyfully give myself unconditionally, only, wholly, and always to your saving grace, O Savior, Lord & Father, AND TO that very same grace poured out to me. However-and through whomever – you appoint to pour it into and pour it out to me – be it in the living donor transplant pathway or be it in any other pathway that lies ahead according to your gracious will."

I ask you to continue to keep me, Sarah, Amy and Ben in your prayers. Prayer is not the least you can do for us, it is indeed the best and most you can do for us. And I ask you to now include the following persons in your prayers: Each person and each of their family members who will deliberate entering the living donor candidacy pathway, and each member of Mayo's LDLT Program staff who will be evaluating the viability of prospective donor candidates.

I thank God for his unwavering grace to me. And I thank God for the grace that you have been and are to me and Sarah and Amy and Ben, and I thank God for all the graces that you have shown and show to me and my family.

And so now I pray with a heart and soul that is truly weller than well the prayer of Psalm 13 first prayed 3000 or so years ago by shepherd-King David to our Savior God:
   "God of Grace, I trust in your faithfulness.
   Grant my heart and soul joy in your help,
That with all of my heart, mind, soul and strength I may continually sing of your love O Lord all my days:
   'Oh how gracious My Heavenly Father is to me!'
Amen

Love, Luther
Trusting Only Jesus and His Grace Always

After a deluge of donor applications were received by Mayo on Luther's behalf, his oldest brother David was chosen for donor screening as the best potential candidate. David was thrilled with the possibility of being a match. He shared his excitement with Luther who was overwhelmed with joy and fear. Luther expressed his concerns to Cindy (David's wife). Cindy's response to him was consoling. What a blessing she is. In Luther's still, prayer-full time, God answered him through Cindy.

From Cindy
July 14, 2003

We are indeed on the same wave length in many respects. In one way, I feel so honored to be allowed to enter your world, feeling the same concern for my husband's health in a similar way that you do about yours. I also have learned that when people ask me about the "how/when" of transplant, I realize that I am only giving a "best guess" and that all of it is within God's purpose, plan and timing. I also know that although God tarries, he is never "late" and that is true regardless of what the outcome of all this is. I try minute by minute not to create timelines, scenarios or anything else that I call "vain imaginings" in my head, but continue to turn them all over to the Lord. If I find myself leaping too far ahead, I find the Spirit pulling me back, ever so gently, and slipping my hand back into the Lord's. Too often I am like a headstrong toddler, wanting to slide out of God's lap, to tear off in a hundred directions, some of which are far too dangerous for me to explore. I am endeavoring to be a better "lap child", content in leaning against his strong chest and arms, secure and safe and at peace in his protection and provision. There is such a calmness and peace that I find myself questioning it ...how absurd is that? I think Satan is trying hard to snatch that peace by trying to convince me that it isn't peace at all, only "denial".

Please know that not only am I "ok" with David's decision, all of us are "ok" with it. Not only that, but every member of our family has asked to be on "the list", hoping against hope, that if David is unable to pass all the screening, that one of us might have the privilege of being "the one" What can life do to us? It is just an eye blink in all of eternity. All of us know where our true Home is. I do not fear death, but more importantly, neither do I fear life, either with or without my beloved husband, as long as I am the Lord's and He is mine. And if by David's life or death, my life or death, or any of my family's life or death, God's perfect plan and purpose is accomplished, and he alone receives the glory and honor as a result, then His will be done. "It is well, it is well with my soul!"

Above all, do not spend any precious emotional energy with undue concern for us or what you perceive to be our sacrifice or suffering. God had been leading us and preparing us for this very moment for all of our lives. We count it a privilege and an honor to be able to share this time in this way with you! I love you and your family (my own God-children!) so very much. Hundreds of people, including those we have never met, are holding us in prayer before the Father. What a comfort to have our burdens lifted by so many brothers and sisters. Already we have heard many testimonies about what Luther's life has meant to people who know of his struggle, yet have never met him and how their personal faith and relationship with the Lord have been strengthened as a result. God is doing great things through His bondservant, Luther, and through you Sarah, his beloved. I could really give you a huge hug right about now.

So, next time you catch yourself again at the foot of the throne, just take a quick peek to your right and left, see the multitude who are joining their prayers to yours, and you'll probably catch a glimpse of me right next to you! Love you forever and ever.

CYN

PS. And when all of this is another chapter in history, we need to celebrate!!!!!!

For we serve a God who is worthy of worship regardless of the circumstances.

"There is no greater love than to lay down your life for a friend/brother."

"Be still. Know I am God." We were still and we knew God is our God. Amen.

Chapter 8

Trust

"But whoever trusts in the Lord is kept safe."
Proverbs 29:25

We were trusting through the hills and valleys of the roller coaster ride. The Mayo Clinic journey continues as we keep in God's arms.

From Luther
August 4, 2003

Dear Sisters and Brothers in Christ Jesus,

"But I trust in you, O Lord: I say, "You are my God." My times are in your hand, deliver me. Let your face shine upon me: save me in your steadfast love. O how abundant is your goodness. Blessed be the Lord, for He has wondrously shown His steadfast love to me when I was beset as a city under siege." Psalm 31
On Friday afternoon, August 1, I got the phone call from the Mayo clinic we've all been praying for. Oh how thankful I have been, am now, and forever will be for every single one of your prayers
* *Good News! My beloved brother, David, has offered himself up as, and has successfully passed the initial*

medical tests to be, my liver transplant donor.

- *Good News! On Wednesday, September 3, I will undergo the exploratory surgical exam that is prerequisite for the transplant surgery.*
- *Good News! Provided that the results of the exploratory exam indicate that the cancer remains contained to the current tumor site, then on Thursday and Friday, September 4 & 5, David will undergo the final medical tests at the Mayo Clinic necessary for him to receive the final approval to serve as my liver donor.*
- *Good News! Provided that I get the green light after my exploratory exam AND David get, the green light after his final tests then he and I have a double-date with the transplant team on Tuesday, September 16!*

Now, given that David and I are in the care of a large medical institution under the Hand of God, these dates are subject to change.

David and his wife, Cindy and Sarah and I are doing daily devotionals together from the devotional resource <u>Streams in the Desert</u>*, by L.B. Cowman. Lo and behold here is "the feast" (Psalm 78:19 "Can not God spread a feast table in the wilderness?" Yes, of course He does! God served up for us on Friday morning in the August 1 entry through the teachings of Mrs. Cowman:*

"Offer yourselves to God, as those who have been brought from death to life."
Romans 6:13

"My child, you can trust the Man who died for you. If you cannot trust Him, then whom can you trust? The Man who loved you enough to die for you can be absolutely trusted with the total concerns of the life he

died to save. Dear friend, trust the Man who died for you. You can trust Him to thwart each plan that should be stopped AND you can trust Him to complete each one that results in His greatest glory and your highest good. You can trust Him to lead you down the path that is the very best in the world for you."

My nurse ended our phone call on Friday with one final piece of good news. It seems that they have been swamped with calls from folks connected to me inquiring about the living donor candidacy process, so much so that my nurse asked me to try and put a stop to the rising flood waters of new inquiry calls! She said that if things don't work out for David to receive final approval to be my donor that there is a long, long list of candidates for them to work through to find another donor. It was a most humbling way for our conversation to come to a close. And so I again say thank you to my dear sisters and brothers in Christ. Thank you for your prayers. Thank you to each of you who deliberated making "the call to Mayo." Thank you to each of you who made that call. Thank you to each of you whose name is now on that long, long list of potential liver donor candidates (names that remain confidential to the Mayo Clinic). Thank you to each of you who prayed for all of those who considered the call.

I ask you to continue to keep my family & David and his family in your prayers. I ask that you give thanks and praise to God for His Amazing Grace in Christ Jesus, all He has done, is now doing, and surely will do for us in the weeks and months to come.

I cannot even fathom what our journey would be like without the grace of your Christian fellowship. I will never be able to fully express what your faith, hope and love mean to me. Perhaps when we all get to Heaven God will bless me with a new language to speak to you all those wondrously grace-full things about you that are too deep for my words in this life to express.

You remain in my thoughts and prayers.
Love the Lord, all you His saints. The Lord preserves the faithful. Be strong, and let your heart take courage, all you who wait for The Lord. Psalm 31

Love, Luther, Sarah, Amy and Ben
Trust Only Jesus Always

From Sarah
Thursday, September 4, 2003- Day of the exploratory surgery at Mayo

Well, today was one of those days that you hope does not come, but it did, and now we go on. Unfortunately, the doctor did not come in with good news. He saw what looked like a suspicious area, a speck the size of a grain of sand. He removed it and it was cancer. There is also an area on the underneath part of his pancreas where it appears the tumor has attached itself. This does not mean that he has cancer of the pancreas, but that the tumor has grown such for it to have reached that far. It is located in an area that he was unable to remove that part of pancreas. The left side of his liver is no longer functioning but the right side has grown to make up that difference. With the side no longer working, that is why they were only able to get one stent in back in July.

Luther, being who Luther is, quoted this Bible verse

as we were by his side, Habakkuk 3:17, "Though the fig tree does not bud and there are no grapes on the vine, though the olive crop fails and fields produce no crops, though there be no sheep in the pen and no cattle in the stalls, yet I will rejoice in the Lord, I will be joyful in God my Savior. The sovereign LORD is my strength, He makes my feet like the feet of a deer, and He enables me to go on the heights."

So for today, we pray for calm, comfort and for God's love to pour down and all around us. Do not worry about what will be tomorrow for tomorrow will have worries of its own. But trust that no matter what may come, God will either give you rest and refuge from your troubles or unfailing strength to handle it. That is my strength for today. I will wait for the Lord for He obviously has other plans for this journey. I may not see or understand it now, but He will not leave us. He will be with us in every breath, tear, waking minute. This I know for sure!!!!!!! I will be in touch.

Love,
Sarah

From David. Luther had requested he write this to explain medically what had happened on the day of the exploratory.

The news we received on September 4th about our dear brother in Christ is as difficult to understand as it is to receive. Luther has asked me to explain the findings such that all may have a better grasp of why he is no longer a candidate for a potentially curative liver transplant.

It is important to know that different types of cancers spread in fairly predictable patterns, and cholangiocarcinoma is no different. The surgeon, Dr. Rosen, discovered two findings, either of which would have made transplant impossible. First, he discovered a small nodule that was implanted on the surface of the right lobe of the liver that proved to be a metastasis from the original tumor. Such a nodule is termed a "sentinel nodule", as it serves as a signal that the tumor has changed its behavior from one content to "stay put" into one that has sent out many "scouts" to establish new colonies of cells distant from the primary site. While no other colonies were visible, it is known from experience that even one such colony represents the "tip of the iceberg" and that the other colonies will eventually grow enough to cause other problems. Transplantation requires the immune system to be suppressed to prevent rejection; unfortunately, this would also allow the renegade colonies to grow and multiply even faster, and the last case would become worse than the first.

Secondly, and even more critically, he discovered that the primary tumor invaded two adjacent structures, the pancreas surface and the duodenum, which is the exit from the stomach, and which cannot be successfully removed and would thereby preclude, in and of themselves, the possibility of transplant. Dr. Rosen stated he felt this condition most likely existed as far back as July 2002 when the original tumor was found. As we have known since the beginning, the various types of scans just are not sensitive enough to accurately define the extent of involvement.

Dr. Gores, the main liver specialist in charge of Luther's care these past 14 months, has suggested a few other options that can be discussed further after Luther has fully recuperated from this surgery, which he equated to that of a "trauma victim". This will gradually abate, and his normal bodily functions will gradually return. At the six weeks check up, further options will be discussed and decisions will be made.

Until then, we encourage each of you to continue to use the prayer calendar to assist your journey of supporting Luther and his family. We know that the prayers of the righteous avail much. Our hope is built on nothing less than Jesus' blood and righteousness. We rest in the knowledge that His Spirit intercedes for the saints according to the will of God, and prays for us all with sighs too deep for words. We claim the promise of II Corinthians 12:9 that His grace be sufficient enough, for each of you, for His power is made perfect in our weakness. For it is then that the power of Christ may dwell in you. May He continue to provide you grace and mercy in your time of need.

In Him, with Him and for Him, David

TODAY I FOUND JESUS IN ROOM 10224
By Pastor Steve Bauerle (Sarah's brother)

*My sister Pam died in January of 2003 of Cystic fibrosis at the age of 43. When I went into her house following her death, I was amazed. I found 8-10 little blue stick-ems with these words written on each one of them, **Today I found Jesus**. One sticker was on her* *television, one was on her kitchen cabinet and one on her counter. One blue-stick-em was in her bedroom and one on the mirror in the bathroom. At first I thought it was a little strange, until I found Jesus in room 10224.*

It was on a Thursday. The date was September 4, 2003 at the Mayo Clinic in Rochester, MN. Jesus' disciples found Him on the beach, walking on the water, healing in a city and transforming on a mountain. My sister found Him in her home. I found Him in room 10224.

My family and I just were informed that my brother-in-law, Luther, had been rejected for a live liver transplant. The news was stunning! Numbing! This news came just a few months after he was rejected for a cadaver liver transplant. My family and I traveled to the Mayo Clinic expecting one of two things; First, that the doctor would perform an exploratory surgery on Luther and tell him he was a transplant recipient, perform the transplant, and after some time of healing at the clinic, he would go back to being the loving husband, caring father, and Christ centered Pastor that he had been before; or secondly, we expected that the doctor would perform the exploratory surgery and tell us that he was NOT eligible, and he would return home and within a few months, die. Little did I know that in the midst of the worst news of my life, I would find Jesus in room 10224.

It seemed like such a long walk from the waiting room to his room. As I was walking, I said to myself, you are the Pastor in the family. What are you going to say to him to minister to him? I was scared wondering what Luther would be like. I had played baseball, football, and swam with him in the Atlantic Ocean. We had talked ministry and theology hundreds of times. He was so athletic and intelligent, yet humble and compassionate. I recall walking past the nurse's station and the nurse looked at me in a way that I did not understand at the time. Now, I am wondering if she saw and found Jesus in room 10224 before I did. It was so peaceful in there where He was. My family and I took turns visiting Luther after hearing of the bad news. I know not only myself, but Luther's brothers, our mothers, and all who were there that day were thinking of ways that we could minister to Luther, Ben, Amy and my sister, Sarah. Yet, we soon discovered that WE were ministered to by Jesus, through Luther.

All of my life I did expect to find Jesus, somewhere, sometime. Yet, I actually expected to be overcome with fear like Moses was. I expected to find Jesus standing before me somewhere in my life but glowing white as Peter, James and John found Him on top of the mountain. Never did I expect to find Him through God's word, his simple word, in the voice of Luther Lee Wright, my brother-in-law, in room 10224 of the Mayo Clinic.

As each one of us walked in room 10224 of the Mayo Clinic, Jesus spoke to us with His word through Luther. For the most part, even without a Bible to read from, Luther began to quote scripture to each member of his family while still under anesthesia! To his mothers, Jean and Bonnie, he quoted Hebrews 4: 14b-16: Let us hold firmly to the faith we profess. For we do not have a priest who is unable to sympathize with our weaknesses, but we have one who has been tempted in every way, just as we are-yet without sin. Let us approach the throne of grace with confidence, so that we may receive mercy and find grace to help us in our time of need. Jesus was there and I found Him! To his daughter, Amy, he quoted Zephaniah 3:17, The Lord your God is with you, He is mighty to save you. He will take great delight in you. He will quiet you with his love, He will rejoice over you with singing. Jesus was there and I found Him! To his son, Ben, Lamentations 3:21-23; This I call to mind and therefore I have hope: Because of the Lord's great love we are not consumed, for his compassion never fails. They are new every morning and great is your faithfulness. I found Jesus! To his wife, my sister Sarah, he quoted Isaiah 40: 27b-28, 31: You say, my way is hidden from the Lord; my cause is disregarded by my God? Do you not know? Have you not heard? The Lord is the everlasting God, the Creator of the ends of the earth. He will not grow tired or weary, and his understanding no one can fathom. He gives strength to the weary and increases the power of the weak. But those who hope in the Lord will renew their strength. They will soar on wings like eagles; they will run and not grow weary, they will walk and not be faint. How blessed I was that again, I found Him. And to me, a man who would soon be married to my wife Amy, he quoted Ecclesiastes 4: 9-10; Two are better than one, because they have a good return for their work. If one falls down, the other helps him up. Pity to the man who falls and no one to help him up! There I recognized Him again. How wonderful the feeling was. How peaceful. Even in the midst of the worst news in my life, Jesus was there! And I found Him.

It was quiet in that room in September of 2003. I now know what King David meant in Psalm 46 when

*he wrote the words, "Be still and know that I am God."
It was still there on that day and I know that God was
there through Jesus. What a peace and comfort His
presence brought to me. King David was tending sheep.
I was sitting by the bed of my brother-in-law.*

*I wrote this chapter for you in order to help prepare you
for when you find Jesus in your life. May it be a time
when you are open to seeing Him. I pray that you are. I
was and it changed my life!*

From Luther to those who traveled to the Mayo Clinic
Thursday, September 11, 2003

*Dear Mom, Bonnie, Dave, Cindy, Rachel, Don, Carol
Ann, Monika, Steve, Kim & Craig,*

*I pray that the Holy Spirit will take my feeble words
and translate them heart-to-heart in such a way that
you can fully comprehend their meaning.*

*And I want you to know that I would have loved to
have been fully able...physically and emotionally...to
speak these words to you in person before we said our
goodbyes in Rochester (at Mayo).*

*I thank God for giving you to me to love and know as
companions in my pilgrimage here on earth AND I thank
Him and you for your love... for your self-sacrifice...
for your presence... for your prayers... for your
compassion... for your support...for your kindness...for
your gentleness...for your encouragement...for your
commitment...for your friendship...for your laughter...
for your songs...for your camaraderie...for your*

wisdom…for your guidance…for your tenderness… for your endurance…for your understanding…for your help…for your patience…for your joy…for your generosity of spirit…for your Scripture recitations… for your faith…your hope…your love…Thank you for being you…Thank you for being there when I needed you most…Thank you for being there when I needed you most to be with my dear Sarah, my precious Amy and my sweet Ben…

"Rejoice always, pray constantly, give thanks in all circumstances; for this is the will of God in Christ Jesus for us." 2 Thessalonians 5:16-18

Love, Luther

Chapter 9

Love, Grace and Mercy Abound

"Peace I leave with you; my peace I give you. I do not give you as the world gives. Do not let your hearts be troubled and do not be afraid." John 14:27

I feel the Holy Spirit deep within me and I am amazed at its power. Love, grace & mercy abound.

The day after what we had hoped would be a transplant, Luther's faithfulness and trust in the man who bled and died for him shone through yet once again. He made reference to a sermon from the African American Pulpit, Spring '99, called 'Resurrection Means Peace.' "God breathed the breath of life to humanity and Christ blew life into the new community made of his blood and broken body." I always try to imagine the disciples up in the room, after He died on the cross; scared, alone, wondering what just happened to their Jesus. The tension was probably thick and hardly anyone spoke. And then Jesus walked in the room and said, "Peace be with you." Imagine that. Peace… the peace that passes human understanding. Jesus breathed that on us. Once you know that peace, you don't forget it. It may get clouded, but not forgotten. It is too strong. For you see, once you GET IT, you want to keep it. You hang onto it because of what it means. Every breath, every word and thought, all that I am is filled with Jesus. I want people to see the Jesus I see and know and love and trust.

From Luther
September 17, 2003

Dear David,

Hope all is going well for you as you get back into the swing of things. Yesterday sure was a weird day, wondering how it was for you…I still can't fathom what your side of this was like, is like. This morning I read a sermon on John 20:19-23 titled, "The Resurrection Means Peace", I came across these words that made me think of you.

"As God's breath gave birth to humanity, so Christ blew life into the new community made of his broken body and blood, his victory over death."

Victory over death? Not when we are sitting by the gravesite watching the pastor throw dirt and flowers on a casket bearing one we love as it is lowered into the earth. I confess something that veers near hypocrisy as I ask that bold scriptural question, "O death, where is thy sting?' I Corinthians 15:55. I've seen and felt death's sting, and survived!

In truth, in time, we come to know that each loved one lives in and through us; death is defeated by the love we bear of them. Love, given and received, is eternal. That is a divine peace, passing our human understanding, soothing our troubled hearts and restless minds. It is a divine gift of the Crucified and Resurrected Jesus.

(So) When Jesus bids the disciples and us, "Go",

and breathes on us, we can go trusting his word because we know his words have come true: "The hour is coming...when you will be scattered, each one to his home, and you will leave me alone...I have said this to you, so that in me you may have peace. In the world you face persecution. But take courage; I have conquered the world" (John 16: 32-33)

In a paraphrase of Anne Lamott in <u>Bird by Bird: Some Instructions on Writing and Life</u>, there is no point in writing hopeless sermons. "We all know we're going to die; what's important is the kind of men and women we are in the face of this."

I want to be like the little boy in a story told by Jack Cornfield and recorded by Anne Lamott. He was eight and had a younger sister dying of leukemia. She would die without a blood transfusion, and his parents told him his blood might be a match. He agreed to let them test his blood, and it was a match. Then they asked him if he would give his sister one pint of blood. He said he would have to think about it overnight. The next day he went to his parents and told them he would give his sister his blood. They went to the hospital, and he and his sister were laid side by side with IVs in their arms. He lay in silence while the blood dripped into his sister. The doctor went over to him to seen how he was doing. He opened his eyes and asked, "How soon until I start to die?"

The dissonance, the persecution, the human face of our sin, these are everywhere around us and in us, there is no escaping that. And yet there is this wondrous truth: I know what that little boy did. He went into the Gethsemane of his bedroom and wrestled with angels while his parents and the world slept, until God called his name, until the peace of God descended upon him. Next morning, his heart filled with love for his sister and God's peace, he courageously got up on that gurney and waited to die. All the dissonance in the world is resolved in his gift. The very world has been conquered.

Can't you feel the very breath of the living God on your face as Jesus says, "Peace be with you"? The resurrection means peace. Let us go into the world bearing the peace of Christ, who is standing in our midst. Let us go into the world in the courage and comfort of the strength of the Holy Spirit. Let us go into the world loving and forgiving the sins of others. In the healing and reconciliation that will follow God's Beloved, the community of Christ that overcomes the world will come to life. Amen

Thanks for being love, faith, hope, peace, joy, grace, mercy and courage to me. What didn't happen yesterday -- can't change that!

And thanks for once again showing me what kind of man that I can be in Christ.

Love You Bro, Luther

Chapter 10

God Makes a Way out of No Way

"Give us this day our daily bread."
Luke 11:3

We had been home for two weeks from the Mayo Clinic after the exploratory surgery. One morning I was leaving to go to breakfast with a friend and to donate blood. I knew Luther was not feeling well, but encouraged by him, I followed through with my plans. I had just begun the donating process when my cell phone rang. My caller ID indicated 'Home Sweet Home' and I knew this was not good. It was Ben calling at Luther's request to have me come home immediately. Luther was so eager for me to spend time with a friend, he would not have called if it were not an emergency. When I arrived home he was in his chair. I fell to my knees in front of him saying we needed to go to the emergency room. With his sad eyes fixed on me he said, "I thought I had more time." My heart was heavy. We feared this was 'it,' but God would make a way out of no way.

In the emergency room, Luther began vomiting. We discovered he was not digesting food. Knowing the tumor had spread to the duodenum, we feared it was being choked off. Tests confirmed our suspicions. During his hospital stay, his primary nurse was an extraordinary woman named Nancy. Her personal pain and suffering had taken her to the oncology unit to help and care for others. God sent her to us and God sent Luther to her.

He was discharged after a few days and told to follow closely the provided liquid diet. This was his new hope and challenge: how to successfully get enough calories and protein to stay nourished. He amazed his doctors at his ability to succeed at this daunting task.

From Luther
September 24, 2003

Dear family and friends,

It is good to be home. Thank you for the bounty of your ongoing flow of prayers and cards. It is God's answers to your prayers that have brought me home to be with my precious Sarah, Amy and Ben, AND keep us trusting and thanking only Jesus always during this difficult stretch of our path.

Taking life a glass at a time right now on my new liquid-delicious diet, I'm blessed to neither be hungry nor craving T-bones, so there is no desperation of deprivation to contend with. Quite the opposite, for I "get to" drink an 8oz cup of "daily bread" each and every hour that I'm awake! The dietitian at the hospital was truly an angel of hope sent by God to counsel and encourage and convince me that the decision to postpone my major duodenum bi-pass surgery and come-home-now-plan was do-able from a nutrition standpoint. She gave me a notebook full of recipes for my cup-an-hour feasts.

Speaking of angels of hope...As my nurse was going over my discharge plans yesterday afternoon she concluded a conversation with me that she had started when she began her shift at 7 a.m. (she has been my a.m. nurse the day before too) by asking me, "So, what kind of work do you do?" I told her that I had served as a Lutheran pastor and was now on disability. She told me that she had been raised Catholic, but as an adult she was not a "practicing Catholic." She then told me that she lived behind a Lutheran Church and that she regularly donated clothes and other goods to that church's social ministry efforts. She said that every time she made a donation, the folks at the church were friendly and invited her to come and worship. She told me she wasn't quite ready to take that step but that when she was that would be the church she'd try. I asked her which Lutheran church it was. It happened to be a church pastored by one of my colleagues. I assured her that she'd receive a warm welcome and strong Gospel messages when she did decide to take that step. With each subsequent time she'd come in to care for me yesterday she'd share a bit more with me about her life. Upon our first nurse-patient contact the previous day, she was very business-like with no interest or time for chit chat (poor woman to be assigned care for the king of chit chat!) And yet there was something in/about her countenance in our first contact that led me to conclude she has suffered some great loss and hurt in her life that was still very much afflicting her.

Fast forward to yesterday afternoon; by this time

we had quite the banter going. And lo and behold as she was going over my discharge orders with me and Sarah (and our dear friend Kath who is a nurse educator at the hospital) she wished us God's blessings for our homeward journey. And then she tells us that the reason she works as an oncology nurse is because in 2000 her then three- year-old son died suddenly of leukemia (previously undiagnosed. He was "healthy" on Thursday, had a fever on Friday and was dead on Sunday. She said that she decided then to dedicate her life to the care of cancer patients and hoped also to be able to work for a cure for cancers. She then said that all her clothing and goods donations to the church were her "Jake Fund"... made gladly in his memory and honor... WOW!!! It was a most amazing and hope-full end to my tough hospital stay, to know that I had been cared for and ministered to by this incredible woman of faith in honor and memory of her beloved son Jake...Amazing grace and fruit-full faith indeed...I give thanks to God for each and every blessing He continually showers upon me through all who care for me...Shepherd-King David had it oh so right when he confesses: "The Lord is good to all, and His compassion is over all that He has made...The Lord is faithful and gracious...He upholds all who are falling, and raises up all who are bowed down. He opens His hand and satisfies the desire of every living thing...He is near to all who call upon Him, He hears our cries and saves us." Psalm 145

I pray that the hope and peace and joy and strength and courage of faith in God will empower you for all you face today that you may beautify God and the lives of others with your love.

I know that my life and the lives of Sarah and Amy and Ben are evermore beautiful because of your great love.

Trusting and praising and thanking and hoping in only Jesus always.
Love, Luther

From Luther
September 27, 2003

Dear David,

When I came out to the living room this morning I saw an email laying on the computer desktop. I looked at it and saw that it was from you to Ben...the one you sent in answer to his questions from the other night. I skimmed it quickly in an effort to see if there was anything either he or you would classify as confidential in it. I figured there wasn't or he wouldn't have left it out where he did! Once I saw that it didn't, I took time to read it. I guess the raw clinical picture always has a chilling effect on the patient (and probably the doctor too, eh?). And so it did once again this morning. As is my custom, I then began my morning with my devotion time turning first to Max Lucado's Grace For The Moment and lo and behold it was on Job 42 and contained Max's essential summary of the message of Job: When you have difficulty tracing God's unfathomable hand, then stick to trusting His heart.

I then turned to L.B. Cowman's Streams in the Desert and lo and behold another Job passage and Cowman's amazing meditation on "divine healing" (would be a heck of a thing to put on the back of your business card or on the back of your prescription sheets). And then I turned to the Gospel of Luke, Chapter 10 (I'm reading through it passage-by-passage day-by-day. On the surface of it, Luke 10 doesn't hold much application to someone in my "clinical position" other than perhaps to make me yearn for the days of pastoral ministry and again repent of every complaint I ever muttered on the mission field. But upon closer look:

1. *What was the mission core of 70s essential commission? v. 9 "heal the sick and say to them, "The kingdom of God has come near to you"...hmm*

2. *v. 17 "The 70 people returned with JOY, saying, "LORD, even the demons are subject to us in YOUR NAME."*

3. *v. 18 and Jesus said to them (with bliss and a nod, I'm sure), "(Don't you know) I saw Satan fall (not falling, but fallen, that is, his defeat is already accomplished!) like lightning from heaven. (Hence) Behold, I have given (done deal) you authority (the authority of everything being subject to MY NAME) to tread over serpents and scorpions (and lions and bears, oh my!); AND OVER ALL THE POWER OF THE ENEMY (OH MY!!!); AND NOTHING SHALL HURT YOU (no never ever!)!*

4. *v. 20 'NEVERTHELESS (as great as THIS NEWS IS and GREAT IT IS!) do not rejoice in this that the spirits are subject to you (because you see it's the means and not the end) but rejoice in this (THIS THE PURPOSE, THE END, THE GOAL OF MY MISSION)...that your names are written in heaven (CAN'T TOUCH THIS!!!)...nothing can separate you from my eternal love, love, love! Absolutely*

nothing can stand in the way of THE ABSOLUTE EVERYTHING JOY THAT COMES WHEN YOU REST IN MY PERFECT LOVE!!! There simply ain't an accomplishment that can compare with THIS!!! This JOY is the same JOY Paul experienced in jail and testified to in Philippians 4: 4!!!

5. *Now David, I've read Luke many times, and I've read this passage many times, but until this morning I never ever saw this next verse: v. 21 "In that same hour Jesus rejoiced in the Holy Spirit: chew on that line for a few minutes! And now the cause for Jesus' rejoicings: God the Son was rejoicing in God the Holy Spirit BECAUSE He was THANK-FULL in His relationship with God the Father BECAUSE God the Father had delivered all things to God the Son so that God the Son could accomplish perfectly and completely God the Father's Will, namely, that the name of every one of God's children should be written permanently in heaven on the heart of God... THUS EN-JOYING for all eternity the ONE-NESS WITH GOD OUR FATHER that God the Father and God the Son and God the Holy Spirit experience and enjoy in the ecstasy and "mystery' of the Trinity. A love relationship in the Trinity that has no beginning and no ending. A love relationship that is un-conditional. A love relationship that is indeed THE GREATEST THING.*

6. *And isn't it a kick to know that Jesus rejoices in the Holy Spirit each and every time and each and every moment God's child "rejoices that my name is written in heaven on the heart of God"?*

From Job to joy thanks to the Holy Spirit.

My prayer for you and each member of your family, Cindy, Tim, Amy, Paul, Jennifer, Madeline, Matthew and Rachel is that the joy and rejoicing of knowing that your names are written in heaven on the heart of God be your delight and strength (Nehemiah 8:10) this day.

I love you my dear brother & friend!
Luther

Chapter 11

The Benefit Magnificent

"I cannot do it alone
The waves surge fast and high,
And the fogs close all around
The light goes out in the sky;
But I know that we two
Will win in the end,
Jesus and I

Cowardly, wayward and weak,
I change with the changing sky;
Today so eager and bright,
Tomorrow too weak to try;
But He never gives in
So we two will win,
Jesus and I

I could not guide it myself,
My boat on life's wild sea;
There's one who sits by my side,
Who pulls and steers with me;
And I know that we two
Will safe enter port,
Jesus & I"

Luther's addition
And so for Sarah and Amy and Ben,

In their grief and mourning;
I know they too will win in the end,
Jesus & Sarah and Amy and Ben.

Streams in the Desert, L.B. Cowman. Zondervan Publishing,
1997. December 21

The benefit team began with just a few people who had come together to share their thoughts on how to give us a helping hand. The bills were mounting only to grow steeper. The few had no idea what God was going to lead them to do.

The outcome: more than 700 people entered the doors and an amazing amount of money was raised!!!! Praise be to God!

From Luther
October 16, 2003

Dear family and friends,
I am doing well. I've been home from my most recent hospitalization for three weeks and I am happy to report that I've been able to maintain my weight on my liquid-soft diet. All the vital liver life-lines still remain open and so if all remains status quo I will begin my new chemo course on 10/22. It will be administered IV once a week for 8 weeks. I will have an IV port installed just below the skin of my upper chest next week. At the end of the first 8 weeks of treatment we should be able to see if it is having its intended effect: to put the cancer into remission and shrink the tumors stranglehold on the various liver life-lines. As long as I am able to receive adequate nourishment via the liquid-soft diet, the plan

*is to leave the duodenum blockage alone in the hope
that the results of the Chemo will make gastric bi-pass
surgery unnecessary.*

*This Saturday the congregation is putting on a
community-wide benefit to collect money to help us
with our medical expenses. The response has been
tremendous...God's graces continue to fill our cup
to overflowing. There will be a catered meal, a silent
auction, organ donation education and registration and
entertainment. It should be a great party! I'm praying
that my health will remain stable so I can celebrate the
absolute goodness of the grace of God with our many,
many friends from Sandusky and Detroit and Lake
Orion; not to mention some family members who will be
coming in for it. Publicists for the event have given me
the opportunity to tell my story and the need for organ
donation in the print and TV media. Here's hoping for
an increase in registered organ donors!*

*LOVE, Luther
Trusting only Jesus always*

October 19, 2003

*Dear Sisters and Brothers in Christ,
    After a good nights sleep Sarah and I awoke this
morning to the very same thoughts and feelings that
filled our heads and hearts and souls as we closed our
eyes last night...that surely we were the recipients of
the most magnificent expression of love the world has
ever known this side of Calvary and Easter and this side
of Christ's Second Coming! Truly, truly, truly you are*

children of the King of Love!

As I struggle to find words to talk about to folks who weren't there yesterday the best I can come up with is to say: From the moment we stepped in the doors to the banquet hall at 3:40 p.m. it was like being swept up in a tidal wave surge of love that carried us to the very horizons of heaven...And that surge didn't ebb when we walked out the doors at 8pm...Nor did that surge ebb when we stepped inside our home...Nor did that surge ebb when we closed our eyes...Nor did that surge ebb when we opened our eyes this morning...Nor has that surge ebbed this noon! And the Holy Spirit weather forecast indicated that there is no let up in this rising tidal surge in the foreseeable future.   I repeat, your love carried us to the very horizons of heaven!

Truly the Father, the Son and the Holy Spirit were present in all God's Glory and God the three-in-one glorified in the grace upon grace upon grace that flowed from your hearts to ours and the love upon love upon love that flowed from our hearts to yours. What a magnificent experience!

If there was even a single unbeliever who stepped over the threshold of the banquet hall coming in, there is no way they could have left without the Holy Spirit singing in their hearts, "Amazing Grace how sweet the sound...I once was lost, but now am found, was blind, but now I see! Jesus I am yours!"

As incredible as the celebration was last night...and of how great was it for Mr. and Mrs. Willet to continue to redeem their son's tragic death by giving sacrificially of their time in love to speak about and staff the Organ Transplant Information Table...it seems more incredible to know that there are proceeds coming from the Benefit to help us zero out our debt at the Mayo Clinic and at Troy Beaumont Hospital and my doctors!

Truly if last night were "all" we had received that would be enough...and far beyond all we could have dared to imagine it could be. And I can honestly say, that if "all" we would have received is the proceed$ without the celebration, then though our material needs would have been met beyond all we could have dared to imagine, it would have still been "immaterial". For by inseparably uniting the spiritual with the material you have truly followed the genius of God who in making His Perfect Word flesh and truly putting His own skin on the Gospel in such a way that His Love, His Grace, His Mercy is frankly irresistible and absolutely accessible to every sinner! You have shown us Jesus and our hearts are glad!

Now as to the timing of the Wright Family Benefit on October 18...Get a Load of this: Thursday, October 16 (brother, David and living donor liver transplant candidate's birthday!) was the end of the 6th full week in my post-surgery recovery period. When I left Mayo on 9/10 I was told that I would have to wait at least 6 weeks post-surgery before I could start the new chemo regimen. Well, on October 16 I called my oncologist and he scheduled me to start chemo on October 22. He told me to contact a surgeon to schedule a day and a time (hopefully he said no later then before my second Chemo treatment on October 29) to have an IV port inserted in my upper chest for the once weekly administration of the chemo. I called the surgeon he referred me to and lo and behold the surgeon could see me that very afternoon for the consultation appointment and he could schedule me for the procedure on Monday, October 20 and therefore I would be good to go for the initial chemo treatment on October 22! All of those dates fitting nicely around my 45th birthday on October 21! Now on top of that get a Load of this: Two weeks ago my mother-in-law gave me a book titled Speaking of Trust Conversing with Luther about the Sermon on the Mount by Martin Marty, Augsburg Fortress Press, 2003. I started reading it on October 9 and from the opening words of Chapter 1..."Therefore," Jesus teaches, "I tell you, do not be anxious about your life, what you shall eat or what you shall drink, nor about your body, what you shall put on. Is not life more than food and the body more than clothing?" (Matthew 6:25)...it was clear that God had put this book in my hand, through my mother-in-law, Bonnie's obedience to the Holy Spirit and her love for me, as my final preparation for the next stretch in the particulars of my trust-only-Jesus-always pathway: the start of a new chemo with all of its hopes and fears, its known and unknowns, its mights and might nots.

And then last night chapter two of Speaking of Trust came to life in our very midst: Jesus teaches, "But seek ye first the kingdom of God and His righteousness, and all these things shall be yours as well." (Matthew 6:33)...And for all you who were part of things last night in person or in spirit these kingdom truths about the sovereign saving activity of God in Jesus Christ were experienced as The Gospel Truth for our lives: The kingdom of God matters most to Jesus and so what matters most to Jesus is that the kingdom of God matters most to us...And what matters most in the kingdom is our relationships...And what matters most in our relationships are matters of the heart... And what matters most in matters of the heart is love, grace, mercy, kindness, compassion, justice, service, honor, forgiveness, reconciliation, generosity, fidelity... All of which combine to make the distinct friendship of Christian brotherhood and sisterhood to simply be love, more love, and more love! And where there is the kingdom of God and His righteousness (our love for Jesus and for one another) this is most certainly true... For we have Jesus' word on it..." **And all these things shall be yours as well.**

My prayer is that your personal, individual, unique experience of the kingdom of God and His righteousness in last night's Magnificent Benefit has given you an equally personal, individual, unique, testimony to share with your own family and friends and co-workers and neighbors about the **"and all these things shall be yours as well"** *promise of Jesus that was most certainly fulfilled in us.*

And I pray that the tidal wave surge of love that continues to lift the Wright family boat to the very horizon of heaven will be a surge that will continue to lift your own family's boat of faith to the very horizon of heaven also!

And what a glorious harbor heaven will be!!! For behold who & what awaits us:

"And I heard a loud voice from the throne saying, Behold, the dwelling of God with His children. He will dwell with them, and they shall be His people, and God Himself will be with them; He will wipe away every tear from their eyes, and death shall be no more, neither shall

there be mourning nor crying nor pain any more, for the former things have passed away." And He who sat upon the throne said, "Behold, I make all things new."

"There shall no more be anything accursed, for the throne of God and of the Lamb shall be in it, and there we His servants will worship Him; we shall see His face, and His name shall be on our foreheads…And the Lord God will be our light, and we shall reign with Him forever and ever." Revelation 21:3-5 & 22:3-5

Yes, what a glorious harbor heaven will be!

All Our Love to Each One of You
Luther, Sarah, Amy and Ben
Trusting and Praising Only Jesus Always

Chapter 12

Second Opinion

"If we are distressed, it is for your comfort and
salvation. If we are comforted, it is for your comfort,
which produces in you patient endurance of the
same sufferings we suffer. And our hope for you is
firm, because we know that just as you share in our
sufferings, so you also share in our comfort."
2 Corinthians 1: 6-7

The journey called cancer has taught us many things;
one of which that the patient is the decision maker as long
as he or she is able. You gather all the needed information,
discuss it with people you love and trust and then make
your decision. We were challenged by the first surgeon
regarding our decision to proceed with the risky gastric
bypass surgery. He reminded us that we could not change
the outcome of the cancer and that 'drawing the line and
crossing it' was foolish thinking. I wanted to share with you
one life line we drew and crossed over to show the hope
and joy we still had in spite of the cancer. Foolish thinking?
I think not. For you cannot live without hope. We looked
for hope each day and found it.

Updates from me
December 4, 2003

I just left Luther at the hospital where he was admitted tonight. Over the past two weeks it has been tough for him. He began by getting sick one week and the doctor thought that maybe the duodenum was plugged by something he ate that was to big. (Quick update---mid September the tumor, which is wrapped around the duodenum, began to choke it off to about one-third of the size. He has been on a liquid, soft diet since mid Sept). He has lost 25 lbs since September 4th. Anyway, he started to be more careful in what he ate trying to keep it pretty thin. Last week, he was sick again. It got to the point where he was only drinking clear liquids. Since last Sunday, he has only been able to drink about 12oz per day. That includes jello and water and other clear liquids. Not a lot for him. He is maybe getting 350 calories per day. On Tuesday they did an upper GI series. He drank the barium and they took pictures to see how it passed through the stomach and on through. WELL----it never left his stomach. He went back Wednesday morning, they took another picture, and still it had not left his stomach. So, the doctor wanted him admitted today to get him hydrated. Tomorrow they will do a scope to see what is what. This is a scary time, knowing the tumor is still growing or least moving enough to further choke off the duodenum, even though he has been on a new chemo for 6 weeks. We are not sure what all of this means. Perhaps we will know more tomorrow. For tonight I leave him in God's hands to care for him and hopefully get a good night's *sleep. I will let you know what tomorrow brings. Thanks for the continued prayers. Love, Sarah*

December 6, 2003

As I begin my day, I remind myself that TOJA (Trusting Only Jesus Always) is probably more important today than it has ever been in my life. Knowing God is present with us in this time I find to be very reassuring.

Luther is still in the hospital. They are hydrating him with an IV. At this particular time he has minimal pain and is not jaundiced, so he is not itching. Praise God for that. Since he has not been able to eat in several days, he said yesterday he feels better than he has in weeks, which I find to be quite ironic. At this point we have few options, any that we do have involve substantial risk and we must ask ourselves if the risks are worth it or is it better to let go at this point and let nature take its course. We have some very tough decisions to make. We have had time to talk with the kids and give them the details, but all of us have not been together in one room yet at the same time to be able to talk as a family. The kids and I are going up to the hospital at 1 p.m. today in hopes of having that time. I will keep you posted on decisions we make and what our next stop is. People ask me if they can do something for us knowing we all feel helpless in times like this. I would ask that you pray to our sweet Jesus for Luther...for calm, peace, love, guidance, hope...for the kids...that God's love showers over them in this and that they are able to see God's loving hand in such difficult times...for me...patience, love, courage, strength, guidance, peace, calm, and to be reminded to

Trust Only Jesus Always in this life, knowing the glory that is to come in the next. Love, Sarah

December 8, 2003

The roller coaster continues tonight. After spending much time speaking with many doctors and time together as a family, we thought today we had made our decision to call in hospice and do a tube in Luther's stomach to release anything that was in there, letting nature take its course. Luther's oncologist wanted us to get a second opinion from a different surgeon regarding the option of the gastric bypass. He felt it was worth having someone else look at Luther's case and decide if the risk was too high or if it would help Luther eat some foods other than clear liquids. This may also buy some more time to continue chemo about five weeks after the surgery. Well, the surgeon, Dr. Renato Albaran, MD, came in and the four of us were able to ask questions and have things explained very clearly. He was very confident that he could do the surgery and that it would be helpful for Luther. He also reminded us that this wouldn't do anything to stop the growth of the tumor in the various places it has spread. This surgery would simply be to increase Luther's nutrition and perhaps build his strength to continue chemo. Such huge decisions. As he was talking I could feel this tremendous pressure thinking "now what do we do?" As he spoke and we asked questions and he took one and one-half hours with us, we are now going to consider this option. The plan would be to let him know tomorrow and he would do it on Wednesday evening. Luther would be in the hospital for about a week and then home for four to five week recovery and then begin chemo again.

So, tonight we place this again in God's hands and hope for guidance and for wisdom and talent of this surgeon who seems so eager to help Luther. I will keep you posted as to our decision. I love you all, Sarah.

December 9, 2003

Well, after much prayer, talking to doctor after doctor and hearing from doctors we trust and feel were very open with us, we have decided to do the gastric bypass. This was such a difficult decision to make. We had a lot of time to talk with the kids and go up and down the roller coaster before going in this direction. We understand that this does not change the cancer in terms of delaying its growth and spread and that this does not mean if the healing process goes well that he will be ready for more chemo. There was more than one doctor who stated Luther is in end stage cancer and that chemo will probably not be an option, but Luther has gone far above and beyond through this whole process. This surgery is meant to help in his quality of life as far as nutrition goes. The hope and goal is that he will be able to eat something other than clear liquids be that protein shakes or eggs or whatever is allowed by the process. And this may be helpful to him nutritionally and psychologically in the time he has left in this life, no matter what that time is. Now, if the surgeon gets in there and finds the cancer has spread too much and it is not safe, he will stop and then place the vent tube in his stomach which will empty his stomach externally. We

will call in hospice and go from there. We all decided this would have been an easier decision if Luther would have looked sickly or was in the itching phase from the Liver breakdown or in much pain. For now he feels really good. We are stepping out on faith and going for it. Please pray for the doctors and nurses and steady hands, for the four of us with peace about the decision regardless of the outcome, and for all of us remember to trust only Jesus always.
Love, Sarah
The surgery will be late tomorrow afternoon or tomorrow evening, depending the O.R. rooms and schedules.

The day began like most, nurses in and out of Luther's room…waiting. Luther and I were talking about his funeral and what he wanted when that time came. To our surprise surgeon #1 came in and asked why we were going ahead with such a risky surgery. "You will cross this line and what? Draw another at January and then February? Your head is in the sand if you think this will change the outcome." Luther very calmly told him he was willing to continue to 'draw the line and cross it' as long as he could. Surgeon #1 obviously did not agree with our decision to proceed with the surgery and made that clear to us. When he left the room, we looked at each other with amazement. Of course we would continue to draw the life lines and cross them. He would too if in our shoes.

Later that afternoon, as we sat together, the four of us, doing some 'Jesus time,' God sent a wonderful gift into the room. Our church friend and nurse educator at the hospital, Kathy, came in with about 15 other hospital employees and a keyboard and sang Christmas carols. They sounded like angels from Heaven. We were deeply touched. When they were done and many of us in tears (Kathy had shared Luther's story with them), we prayed. They left the room and Luther, Amy, Ben, and I looked at each other, calm, filled with hope, love, and peace and agreed... WE ARE READY.

December 11, 2003

Praise God!!!!! The surgery went as planned. They took Luther back about 4:30 and started his epidural. The surgery started about 5 p.m. and took him about one and one-half hours to complete it. The surgeon came and spoke to us about 7:30 p.m. and said he was unable to look on the liver side because there was scar tissue. He did not want to create a problem by disturbing it. He told us he was cautiously optimistic because things went how he planned. He said we would just have to wait to see if the eating thing was going to go smoothly. It will take a few days before they try anything. Luther knew we were all there and that things went well, but he was pretty drugged. They brought him up to his room at 10 and I left him at 11:30. The nurses will check him frequently and will call me if anything changes. I must say it is odd leaving him there with so many tubes and things. Like my Mom said to me yesterday...I have put you in God's hands and you are safe there. That has stuck with me all day and I know it to be true tonight. We will go back tomorrow for the day and take it minute by minute rejoicing in this step and going to the next. We felt your prayers and thoughts and we love you all. Sarah.

Dr. Albaran, MD came out to give me, Amy, Ben, Doa & Carol Ann the good news, it was like music to our ears. We listened eagerly to his hopefulness. When he was done speaking, we all stood. Don looked at him and said "this is from Luther" and gave him an enthusiastic hug. Ah the elation!

All is well…all is well…all is well.

<u>Streams in the Desert:</u> December 13: If you seem to be living in deep darkness because God is working in strange and mysterious ways, do not be afraid. Simply go forward in faith and in love, never doubting Him. He is watching and will bring goodness and beauty from all of your pain and tears.

From Sarah
December 11, 2003

All I can say is that it seems to me that the more tubes Luther has to contend with the more amazing he is. He had a good day today. The surgeon and the gastroenterologist are quite pleased with things thus far. He sat in a chair and walked for 10 minutes at two different times today. (The nurses were thrilled they were not having to tell him again and again to get up and the importance of getting up and moving. I told them to get ready because they will probably have to tell him to slow down. They liked that.)

The pain meds are working great. It was a day of joy and relief just knowing the surgery was done and so far things are going as expected. Not as late a night, but feeling so grateful. Thank you again for your prayers

and thoughts.
Love
Sarah

I got up on the morning of the 11th filled with relief and hope and delight. I called the high school to speak with the social worker who, on occasion, had been checking in with Ben. I wanted to fill him in on the surgery and where things were heading at this point. He began the conversation asking me if I had heard about the baseball coach. Since Ben had played ball throughout high school, I wasn't quite sure which coach he was referencing. He told me all of the boys were in the office being told that the pitching coach had been on his tread mill the night before when he collapsed and died of a heart attack. I was speechless. How was I going to tell Ben the coach he loved working with and respected and admired had just died, AND just after the surgery on his dad the day before? I ended the call by telling the social worker that I would speak to Ben. I woke him, my heart heavy, and told him the sad news I asked if he wanted to go to the school and be with the team. He did not feel he could do that on that morning. We sat together for awhile, holding each other with nothing to say. Later, Ben was able to speak with the head coach, who listened and comforted him. What a mixed-bag-of-emotions day it was.

December 16, 2003

I left the hospital a little early today to try and catch up on some R and R. Luther is doing very well. The N/G tube came out last night and the epidural came out this afternoon. Soon the only tube he will have is an IV.

He is really looking forward to a nice long shower. To make that experience even greater, maintenance came in today and put in a new shower head. He gets up and walks several times a day and sits in the chair for most of the day. He is quite a spunky guy. They started clear liquids today and he said it tasted like a feast. Tomorrow they will start heavier liquids and on Wednesday a soft diet. (I bet that will be the best egg he has ever eaten.) Hopefully he will come home on Wednesday. YEAH!!!!! His incision looks great and really adds to the other incision scar from the exploratory surgery.

This weekend two of his good friends from 2nd grade through high school surprised him with a visit. He was stunned. They flew in from Florida and Atlanta. It was a time filled with much laughter and fun. Luther was quite touched and said he will never forget it. It was wonderful. Our kids enjoyed hearing stories about him as a kid. The weekend was quite a blessing for all of us.

These last few days since the surgery have been blissful. Amazing what a glimmer of hope and quality of life can bring. Thank you for your constant prayers and love. It has been felt deep in our souls. TOJA!!!!!
Sarah

1979
Luther & Sarah dating, Sarah's
first time in Florida.

Luther was always a kid at heart.

Aug. 8, 2001
Luther &
Sarah

May 1, 2004
Luther &
Ben

Christmas
2002
Amy gave all
of the family
rings with
T.O.J.A.
engraved.

2003
Christmas

2003
The Benefit

2003
Christmas
Renewing
our vows.

Late June,
2004

June, 2005
Ben's High School
Graduation
all wearing T-shirts
w/ Luther & Ben
at a baseball
game!

Aug., 2004
Sarah, Amy, & Ben in
Florida to spread
Luther's ashes in
the ocean.

Chapter 13

Rejoice

"Rejoice in the Lord always again, I say rejoice."
Philippians 4:4

Luther was always a wonderful and thoughtful gift giver. Christmas of 2003 was no different. After his most recent surgery, Luther was discharged from the hospital just one week before Christmas. Unbeknownst to me, he had a holiday surprise planned for the three of us. First, he had Ben take him to a jeweler where he had a special gift designed for me. The following day Amy drove him to several florists with our wedding picture in hand in order to have my bouquet remade. He finally came to a florist on the outskirts of town that was willing to recreate it so close to Christmas.

That year it was just the four of us on Christmas morning. After we had opened all of our gifts, or so we thought, Luther had us put on the clothes we wore to church the night before. We were puzzled by his request, but excited. We were, of course, dealing with Luther and surely he had something amazing up his sleeve. He set the video camera in place and let the surprises began to unfold. Luther gave me a large gift bag first. In it was my wedding veil which he placed gently on my head. Next another large bag to open. Inside I found my beautiful wedding bouquet recreated in silk. I began crying tears of great wonder at his love for me. Amy received a gorgeous heart necklace with two diamonds and one sapphire (the gem of hope). The diamonds represented her and him as father and daughter. Ben was given a gold band with two diamonds and a sapphire representing him and Luther as father and son. These gifts are to be worn at special events in their lives that he will not be present at. My gift…a gold necklace with '1TL1': Luther is my one True Love and I am his one True Love. How perfect. How special. How loving. When we finished putting on our new jewelry, Luther presented us with a booklet. Printed on the front of it were the words: 'The renewal of wedding vows of Luther and Sarah Wright'. My heart flooded with many emotions. My sobs were deep and the love and tenderness I felt for and from Luther were immense. There we all stood, the video running, Amy as maid of honor and Ben the best man, drawing a beautiful life line and celebrating as we crossed it that morning. The ceremony was just as special and memorable as our original one on June 14, 1980. I wore my veil for the rest of the day. Our dear friends came by for our annual Christmas morning visit and they were greeted by the renewed bride and groom. What a glorious day.

I share this with you to give you hope for this life and the joy that can be found even in the gloom of cancer. Love abounds and God's faithfulness is new every morning.

December 17, 2003

HE'S HOME!!! HE'S HOME!!! ALL IS WELL!

Love, Sarah

Ho! Ho! Ho! From Luther
December 18, 2003

Dear family and friends

It is so good to be Home Sweet Home with Family Sweet Family! Thank you for all your prayers and visits and calls and cards and gifts, gracious considerations one and all...during my hospitalization and surgery. Your love and compassionate expressions of support buoyed our spirits individually, and our collective spirit as family.

My surgeon and gastro doc tell me that the surgery was very successful. They told me to gradually step my diet up from soft goods to regular goods. While they told me to steer clear of certain hard to digest foods, I now will have a variety of solid foods to once again sink my teeth into for the first time since mid-September. Both docs told me to use and enjoy my new stomach-small intestine anatomy to the fullest! This "more-better" nutrition promises to improve my quality of life by allowing us as a family to sit down at the table together again, and by improving my strength and stamina. While I was counseled not to make my decision to have surgery on the hope of returning to chemotherapy, my view is that if my new and improved diet puts me in a position to resume chemotherapy in due time, I'd certainly like to go for it once again. That will be a decision for a later date. For now I'm enjoying the simple decisions of selecting what I want to eat for dinner tonight. My selections: chicken noodle soup, Kentucky Fried Chicken's mashed potatoes and gravy, and a chocolate milk shake...

YUM! Already looking forward to tomorrow's breakfast decisions.

Ben took me out Christmas shopping for a short bit this afternoon and Amy and I have a date for another short trip tomorrow.

Sooo, it is good to be home and once again Living Large in the joy of the Lord by the grace of God... Trusting only Jesus always...Seeking to live well, laugh often and love much...always with thanksgiving for each of you and for your love and prayers.

I wish for you a very Merry Christmas and a Happy New Year

God bless us every one!

Love, Luther

Chapter 14

Joy vs. Happiness

"So do not fear, for I am with you; do not be dismayed,
for I am your God. I will strengthen you and help you;
I will uphold you with my righteous right hand."
Isaiah 41:10

God's purpose in all things is for us to continue to trust him only in everything. He knows our needs and sometimes we need to be reminded of our need for our God. He is true and faithful and will not fail us.

Luther sent this next email to David in response to a letter David had sent Luther about a friend, Dottie, whose husband had died suddenly.

Luther defines the difference between joy and happiness; a meaning that helps us to understand how there can be joy amidst the sorrow (in Luther's words…shit). He opens his heart beautifully about grief as the griever himself, but also about others in grief. The splendor of it is his honesty.

When we think of our relationship with God, we can come to Him with complete honesty. He already knows our hearts, everything about us. What a gift we have to be able to pour it all out on Jesus. To know we can completely trust Jesus always, what a relief! We don't have to carry our burdens, Jesus does. We don't have to be filled with despair, Jesus died and rose again for that. We don't have to be lonely, Jesus promises never to leave us or forsake us. He knows us completely. The greatest gift is to know Him, too.

December 20, 2003

Dear David,

I commend you for trusting and obeying the prodding of the Holy Spirit by writing the letter to your dear sister, Dottie…Your courageous friendship/brotherhood with Dottie brought to mind this morning's devotional verse: "Every good action and every perfect gift is from God. These good gifts come down from the Creator of the sun, moon, stars and galaxies, who does not change like their shifting shadows." James 1:17.

I read your letter and have no theological "edits" to add or delete from it…Some of my reflections-responses to what you wrote include: About the meaning of JOY, I too differentiate Joy from happiness and do so from the perspective the Joy is unconditional, non-circumstantial, irrevocable, irreversible, and eternal… Whereas happiness is conditional, circumstantial, comes and goes, and is transitory.

Joy and happiness are both gracious gifts of God. Ain't life grand in those moments when we sense we have it all on both accounts! I guess I'd differentiate the two this way: Joy is given to us purely, absolutely in terms of having our faith relationship with God as Savior by grace alone just for the sake of the relationship in which He delights to abide in us and in which He delights that we abide in Him AND when we delight that He abides in us and in which we delight that we abide in Him. Happiness on the other hand is tied to our relationship with the many, many great and good things that God can graciously give to us as Father, Lord, King, Shepherd, etc.

As with our Loving God's gifts of hope and peace, joy is by grace alone through faith alone.

On the subject of joy, my heart, mind and soul were turned to Isaiah 54, during one of my devotional readings in the hospital. Over the long weekend two weeks ago, when I was adrift about what decision trusting only Jesus always would lead me, lead us to, Isaiah 54 is part of what scholars refer to as Second Isaiah...Is. 40-55...and it is God's message of hope addressed to Israel while in exile in "hopeless captivity" in Babylon post 587 B.C. As such it is full of the Old Testament Gospel of Hope. Isaiah 54 is a Song of Assurance to Israel that her future was not barren as it seemed to the naked eye. The image of being barren is a key one in the Old and new Testaments. I imagine it is a potent image for you as a physician given the "barren" couples you have offered fertility counsel and referral over your 25 years of medicine---I know that as a Pastor it is one of the most cancerous forms of hopelessness I ever ran into in the parish. I now know that to be barren of hope is the worst thing one can experience in the human condition. For that was my anguish 7/02 when I was told that my cancer was inoperable and incurable. That was my anguish when told about the cadaver waiting list. That was my anguish when told I needed to go the route of living donor. That was my anguish on the evening of 9/4/03. That was my anguish two weekends ago. To come to the point where I thought that my slim hopes had finally run out. To have to accept the cancer of such hopelessness was surely a fate worse than death. And to know how destructive that cancer of hopelessness would have been for each member of the family. Little wonder I opted for surgery even with its risks and perhaps limited benefits. And oh how palpable hope was when at last I made the decision (And from what I heard hope made quite a commotion when it left the surgeon's lips to the family post surgery)

Returning to the subject of grief and hopelessness. There is something to the condition of barrenness and grief and loss, expressed these ways: I will never again experience _____. I will never again find _____.

I will never again be able to _____.

For those mourners who grieve the barrenness that comes with loss, careful attention to their words and feelings and perceptions of barrenness and hopelessness is a key for care-givers...And oh how beautiful to read in Isaiah 54 these words: "Sing, O barren one. Burst into song and shout!" Why? Because God is not barren. Jesus is alive. Easter announces that the Devil at his worst is no match for God at His Best! God is always pregnant with possibilities for those who are barren! Ain't it interesting that there is not one Bible story on barrenness where the barrenness wasn't overcome!!!

As the old hymn puts it, "there is no other way to be happy in Jesus but to trust and obey (only Jesus always)". Trust that God wills to bring the barrenness to an end with the gift of new life...obey God as you stay in His Word of Hope and walk hopefully with Jesus through the grief in the confidence of patient expectation...

Here's the irreducible minimums of my theodicy (one of Luther's favorite sayings which means the problem of good and evil): Shit happens...But not for a moment does God abandon us to the shit or in shit, fact is He became flesh and entered into the shit...And God never leaves us in the shit...His love, grace, mercy, kindness and love overcomes all the shit...Shit yeah!

And finally I must bring this all to a close. So why not with that which is most personal to me? For I too am both a great hoper and a great griever. Even as I live with God's breath in my body and His spirit in my soul. Mourning the loss of what will never be...with wife and children, mother and sisters and brothers...nieces and nephews...friends...etc...etc

I think it is critical for all grievers to develop a mission-purpose statement for their mourning period. We each must come to terms with our time of grief as a meaning-full period in our lives that is anything but as nonsensical and unreal as it can feel and it seems at times.

Here my dear brother David is my personal statement. You can share it with Dottie for pastoral purposes. I wrote it out and presented copies of it to Sarah and Amy and Ben on October 21. If Dottie proceeds with this endeavor I would encourage her to also share it with the most significant persons in her life.

"The one who has a why for life can put up with any how."
-Friedrich Nietzsche-

"The why for my life, by definition of the Gospel of Jesus Christ, is unconditional love.
The whos for my life, by definition of the Gospel of Jesus Christ, are: God the Father, Son and Holy Spirit

&

all other human beings who are my sisters and brothers in the one family of God

&
myself.
These three, not in a competitive hierarchy, but in a round circle dance of love where there is no beginning and no end, no first, and no last...
Just love, love, love.

You my precious Sarah, Amy and Ben are my primary whos...
Each of you as individual and eternal gifts & sacred trusts from God...
The 4 of us collectively as a family unit an eternal gift and sacred trust from God...
And it is the awesome dignity and sheer delight of unconditionally loving you as my primary circle dance partners and being unconditionally loved by you that is my primary why...

And it is knowing the why and the whos for life which will determine the faith-hope-love attitude with which I will choose to deal with the whats, hows and wheres of my life..

The why and the whos for life are,
by definition of the Gospel of Jesus Christ,
eternal, permanent, changeless,
unconditional, uncircumstantial, essential, non-
negotiable;
The whats, hows and wheres of life are,
By definition of the Gospel of Jesus Christ
temporal, transitory, changing,
conditional, circumstantial, non-essential, negotiable

Trusting only Jesus always,
I pledge to God
&
to you, my Sarah, Amy and Ben
I will delight in each one of you
as we get to fulfill the one why of life with one another
within our circle of love
no matter the whats, hows or wheres that are to come
outside the circle.

October 21, 2003

Well, that's all the news that's fit to print tonight! Love Ya Bro!!! Luther

Chapter 15

Beloved Amy

"The Lord your God is with you, he is mighty to save.
He will take great delight in you, he will quiet you with
his love, he will Rejoice over you with singing."
Zephaniah 3:17

I am Luther's only daughter. He will always be the number one man in my life. There really is no way to describe him and his amazing impact in words, but I am going to try.

He was the kind of father everyone should be blessed to have. I never doubted that I was at the top of his priority list. He was a very 'hands on' pastor and devoted to his church, but always made it a point to be home for dinner, take us to the park and help me with my homework (although those were not always our happiest moments). He built doll houses with me (how many other dads do you know who would spend months building a doll house with his daughter?). He never missed a soccer game or a gymnastics meet. In fact, in 7th grade, I had a major competition and he passed up a chance to meet President Clinton to be there for me. It meant the world to me and I didn't even have to ask him to do that.

My dad made me laugh harder than anyone. He had a sense of humor about him that made you roll your eyes and laugh hysterically at the same time. He gave the best advice and whenever I would come to him with even the pettiest 'boy' problems, he was all ears and always so understanding and compassionate. He made sure I knew how much I was worth and how much I meant to him. Looking back, over all he said to me and all he did for me, I realize more than ever how much my daddy really did love his baby girl.

I miss him more than I thought I could possibly miss anyone. The life and presence he had about him was definitely something that is not easy to live without.

He taught me so many lessons for life. He taught me to be kind and gentle and loving to myself and to those around me. He taught me to never lose faith in God because He is always there with the utmost grace and love. He also taught me that we are all equal: color, age, race and gender. He taught me to never accept anyone or anything that doesn't treat me like the amazing child of God that I am. He taught me to look for the good and always keep my sense of humor, especially during the difficult times. He taught me to be compassionate and understanding and most of all, he taught me to TRUST ONLY JESUS ALWAYS.

He not only taught me these lessons, he lived them. He was the kind of person I pray to be one day. All of his actions and words reflected love. What more could you ask for in a dad? He woke up every morning of his life with a mission to look for all of the beauty and blessings that so many of us take for granted. He treasured every moment and made every one of them count. The joy he claimed in his heart was contagious and genuine.

I know he is still with me every day, helping to guide me down every path. I was so blessed to have this incredible man as my father.

Chapter 16

Leap, Leap, Leap…Faith

"Abide in me, and I in you. As the branch cannot bear fruit by itself, unless it abides in the vine, neither can you, unless you abide in me." John 15:4

We came away from December with the gastric bypass a great success. Luther was able to eat and had taken up the joy of bologna and peanut butter sandwiches: a childhood favorite.

He again started chemo. It was tough on him. You know the saying "sometimes the cure is worse than the disease."

When you can't get out of it; when you can't be delivered from it; then you are left with the first and best option: ABIDE IN HIM. John 15: 4

Jan. 1, 2004
From Sarah

Happy New Year to all of you. Last night, as the ball dropped and it was 2004, Luther and I felt very blessed to have crossed that line together. Never knowing the future, we weren't sure what this day would bring. Let me tell you it is glorious!!!! I have been filled with much joy since deciding to do the surgery and things having worked as well as they have. To celebrate…Luther came home at 138 lbs and is now at 144!!!! Truly something to celebrate as we begin this new year. Everything he eats goes down well and he savors every bite. So for today, which is all we have anyway, we live well, laugh often and love much enjoying each day together and trusting only Jesus always!!!!

Happy New Year 2004!.

Love, Sarah

January 22, 2004
From Luther

Dear Family and Friends:
Just a quick note to let you know that I restarted my Chemotherapy today after an eight week hiatus due to that roller coaster ride in December. The doctors are amazed that I am on a regular diet and consuming enough for two teenage boys. I tipped the scales this morning at 154 lbs, up from 138 lbs on December 9. I've been taking the dog on a two to three mile walk through the woods nearly every day. My Oncologist is hoping to increase the potency of my chemo in a few weeks. As it looks right now, I'll receive Chemo IV once a week for three weeks and then have a rest week off. The plan is to stay on that treatment course as long as I'm able to tolerate it and not have a significant reduction in my quality of life.
"Jesus has taught me:
Relationships matter most in the Kingdom of God…
And that matters of the heart matter most in

relationships...And that love matters most in matters of the heart.

Thanks for all the love you have for us and have shown us. I want to thank each and every one of you for your prayers and support for me and Sarah and Amy and Ben. I pray that this be a most blessed New Year for us all.

Love, Luther Trusting only Jesus Always

January 31, 2004: From Sarah

Dear David,

Luther had his 2nd chemo on Wednesday and they increased the dose. His tumor marker was up, not sure of the number. This round has been tough on him. His platelets were low, so he needed an injection on Thursday. Since then he has been running a temperature that went as high as 100.8 and tremendous pain. Yesterday we saw Dr. Quallich who said it could be chemo, cancer or surgery or all three. He gave him the duragesic patch. When we got home his pain went to a 10. Kind of scary. Chest and back pain between the shoulder blades. I gave him morphine, which did nothing. I called Dr. Q. who called in cipro and flagyl which we were to start and also the patch and vicodin every four hours if needed. The pain lasted three to four hours. He did not want to get in the car to drive to the hospital, so we waited to see what would happen. Things did settle and he had quite a buzz last night. But at least he was relaxed and feeling better. We went to see my Mom in Toledo today (one year today that Pam, my sister, died) and his pain started again on the drive home, but not as bad. We were just 15 minutes away from home when he vomited in the van. Somehow, he found a plastic bag and it worked well. His pain was much better after that. So one asks oneself…what is that from? Meds? Antibiotics? Cancer now around the intestine attached to his stomach? All of the above? For now he is feeling better and continues the meds and we wait and see. I guess the TOJA thing is in full swing for now. What else is there to do but trust and wait? I love you and PLEASE kiss Madeline, your sweet grandbaby, for us. Sarah

And The Miracles Continue

The first ground breaking for the new addition at King of Kings was in April 2002. Luther became ill in July of 2002. Without a full-time pastor, the loans were taken off the table. However, King of Kings would not take 'no' for an answer. By trusting only Jesus always, God provided a way for the building to double in size and be refurbished. As ill as Luther was feeling the week prior to the dedication, it was miraculous he was able to attend and celebrate God's goodness. As you read the dedication letter from Luther, hear the joy and hope that fills it and be reminded that there is nothing too impossible for our God.

Luther's email after the dedication.
March 9, 2004

Dear Sisters and Brothers in Christ Jesus our Risen Savior, Reigning Lord and Ever –Living Friend,

"It is a great day to be King of Kings Lutheran church!" I hope that this acclamation of thanksgiving is a standard chorus in your morning devotion time with God each and every day. I know that my day is just not the same if when counting my blessings and naming them one by one I fail to acclaim the blessing of being a member of King of Kings Lutheran Church with a hearty, "It is a great day to be King of Kings Lutheran church!"

And so what a joy it was on February 29, 2004 to be able to once again be in the midst of the whole congregation and call out to our God in Highest heaven, "It is a great day to be King of Kings Lutheran Church!" And oh what a privilege and honor and joy to be all but knocked off my perch on the ladder with your thunderous response, "It is a great day to be King of Kings Lutheran Church!"!

February 29, 2004 – a great day indeed to be King of Kings Lutheran Church! After more than a decade of visioning and dreaming and waiting and praying and pleading and hoping and waiting and praying and planning and sacrificing and saving and meeting and waiting and praying and worshiping and working and serving and praising and waiting and praying, the whole congregation gathered in the holy name of the Most High God who raised Jesus from the dead to dedicate the Christian Education Center to the great and glorious purposes of God.

As you reflect back on the grace and joy and hope and excitement of the day as you reflect back on the "my cup runneth over" fullness of all your emotions… Now imagine someone adding to all that the astounding surprise of attaching your name to that Christian Education Center. If you can imagine that, then you will know what it is I felt when the curtain on that surprise for me was rolled back by my son Ben at precisely 10:53 AM when, as is his usual custom upon settling into his seat, he counted the pages of the Dedication Sunday bulletin with a teenager's how-long-is-this-service-going-to-last?-sigh-for mercy!!, and came to the next to the last page-page 10, and after scanning the "Order of Dedication" spotted the phrase, "we dedicate this new addition, The Luther Wright Christian Education Center", and then elbowed me with his left arm and pointed to it with his right hand with a smile for the ages spreading from ear to ear!

Imagining all this…Cup running over and over with the highest awareness of God's grace upon mercy rampaging through my entire heart, mind, soul, body and tear ducts like water does when there's a water main break…Imagine adding all this to the first joy of the morning which was opening my eyes and gently shaking my limbs and being aware that once again by the surpassing grace of God I was alive in body and fully alive in Christ Jesus, and not just fully alive, but blessed instantly with the before-I-got-out-of-bed knowledge that God had made me well enough in body and mind and spirit on February 29, 2004 to be able to go to church. Imagine the jig I danced as I got ready for church that morning singing with the Psalmist, "I was glad when they said to me, Let us go unto the house of the Lord and worship Him!"

As I look back on February 29, 2004 as the great day it was to be King of kings Lutheran church, my personal and congregational reflection is shaped by the calendar…February 29, 2004 was Leap Day of the 366-day Leap Year…"The extra day that comes every fourth year in the Gregorian calendar intercalated to compensate for the quarter-day difference between an ordinary year and the astronomical year "(Thank you Webster's Dictionary!) What a wonderful day for this congregation to dedicate this particular new facility given the leap-of-faith upon the grace of God upon leap-of-faith upon the grace of God upon leap-of-faith upon the grace of God we had to take to complete this God-ordained facility in God's way, in God's time, with God's appointed resources when fear and reason and caution and all worldly counsel argues so persuasively and so indefinitely, "Postpone re-applying for the loan until (you fill in the blank)_____. "Postpone Groundbreaking II until (you fill in the blank)_____. "Postpone the start up of construction until (you fill in the blank)_____."

May everyone who, with eyes of faith, ever reviews the various time lines for the construction of this new facility never ever say that it was mere coincidence that the Dedication Sunday for this new facility just so happened to fall on Leap Day 2004 with Leap Day 2004 just happening to fall upon a Sunday and with the building just happening to be completed and prepared for dedication on Leap Sunday 2004. May every one who, with eyes of faith, ever reviews the various time lines for the construction of this new facility always and forever see and say that Leap Sunday February 29, 2004 was divinely writ as The Dedication Sunday as the magnificent exclamation point to the personal signature of God attesting to one and all His providential loving care for King of Kings Lutheran church and the community we serve!!!

And now to the second aspect of the calendar that shapes the way I will forever behold the Leap Sunday Dedication Event of February 29, 2004. For those of you who have become members of King of Kings since I went on medical leave in July 2002, let me begin by introducing myself as a sports fan in the fullest sense of the word "fanatic". As such I know my brain functions in ways that non-sports fanatics brains do not function, and do not care to function! That said, as I sit here in the month of March and reflect back on the honor of having the new facility dedicated to the glory of God and His glorious purposes as The Luther Wright Christian Education Center...And as I reflect back on the wonder of both the privilege and the ability to climb the ladder and raise the dedication plaque into place...And as I reflect on the absolute love, grace and joy that flowed from your smiles to mine, and from my smile to yours... And as I reflect on the way all that love from God to us spontaneously gave way to a flow of unscripted words "about there not being anything too wonderful, too hard, too impossible for out God to do!!!!"* pouring forth from my heart from high upon that ladder-pulpit the best analogy I have to convey all of this when talking about it with others who were not there in person that day is to turn to the image that casual sports fans and fanatics (and their spouses too perhaps!) everywhere will focus on this month throughout the national college basketball tournament that is simply known as "March Madness". That of every member of championship team *climbing the ladder one by one, usually Head Coach first all the way through the players and staff down to the proverbial water boy, to cut down the nets of victory as the most-cherished prize of team whose mission is accomplished for all the world to see!*

So far this is both the only and best image I can behold to make sense of the high honor you bestowed upon me with my place on our ladder, and my name on our building dedication plaque for King of Kings Lutheran Church dedication Sunday, Leap Sunday, February 29, 2004. As one privileged to serve as Pastor of King of Kings and in that regard as "Head Coach & water boy" for just a little while in God's providential building scheme for this new facility…As just one among many Pastors – "Head Coaches & water boys" used by God in the visioning and completion of this project…As just one among the many, many, many team leaders and members…I was humbled to be designated to represent each of you that day high upon that ladder as I placed the plaque/ "cut down the net", just as I was humbled to have my name designated on that plaque to represent each and every name of each and every championship team member who contributed to our beautiful facility. For that special honor, for that humble privilege I say to each and every team member, "Thank you. And to God alone and to His Eternal Purposes be the glory.

Glory to the Father as March Madness becomes Mission Madness! And so on February 29, 2004, the first day of the first week of March 2004 we boldly exclaimed in the Call to Worship: "King of Kings Lutheran Church Lake Orion, Michigan declares to the entire world:

Saved by grace through faith we are transformed

by God's love, which we experience in the presence of Jesus.

Transformed by God, we joyfully devote ourselves to Jesus.

Transformed by God and devoted to Jesus, We commit to share Jesus with everyone so that they too can experience the transforming love of God by the power of the Holy Spirit.

Our vision: We begin to transition immediately to become ever more fully a "Purpose Driven Church". In this way we will live out our commitment.

"The Purpose Driven Church in one sentence: A Great Commitment to the Great Commandment and the Great Commission of Jesus will grow a great church.

Glory to the Son Jesus the Christ as March Madness becomes Mission Madness! And so on February 29, 2004, the first day of the first week of March 2004 we prayed in the Order of Dedication Prayer: "Blessed Lord God, give us joy in all your works, and grant that this place of ministry may always be a place where Your Will is done and Your Name is glorified: through Your Son, Jesus Christ our Lord, who lives and reigns with You and the Holy Spirit, one God, now and forever, Amen."

Glory to the Holy Spirit as March Madness becomes Mission Madness!! And so let us now repeat The Dedication Commission we were sent out into the mission field with on February 29, 2004, the first day of the first week of March 2004:

M. The joy of the Lord is our strength! Go in peace. Serve the Lord.

C. THANKS BE TO GOD!

As we continue to serve Him on the Mission Field may we remember always to rejoice that absolutely nothing is too wonderful, too hard, too impossible for our God to do!* For God is love, God is alive, and God is able! He is our hope for today. And He is our hope for tomorrow. Thanks be to God indeed!

- *These verses were suggested reading by Luther if the time came where he could not do his own reading. We read them all to him.*
- *Genesis 18:14, Genesis 22: 1-7, Exodus 14:30-15:21, Numbers 11:23, Joshua 3, Joshua 21: 43-45, Judges 6-8, I Samuel 17, II Samuel 22, I Kings 18, II Kings 2: 9-12, II Kings 4: 1-37, II Kings 5: 1-15, II Chronicles 20: 1-30, Job 19: 25-27, Psalm 23, Psalm 130, Isaiah 9: 2-7, Isaiah 25: 6-10. Isaiah 35: 1-10, Isaiah 40: 27-31, Isaiah 43: 1-2, Jeremiah 31: 31-34, Lamentations 3: 21-26, Ezekiel 37: 1-14, Daniel 3, Daniel 6, Micah 7: 18-20, Zechariah 4: 6-7, John 1: 14-19, Luke 1:37, Luke 2: 8-20, Luke 4: 18-21, Luke 5: 17-32, Luke 7: 11-22, Luke 8: 40-56, Luke 9: 28-36, Luke 15: 7, John 11: 1-57, John 13: 1-38, Luke 18:27, Mark 9:23, Mark 10: 27, Mark 14:36, Matthew 26-28, Mark 14-16, Luke 22-24, John 18-21, Acts 1:3-11, Acts 2: 1-24, Romans 3: 23-25, Romans 5: 6-8, Ephesians 1: 17-20, Ephesians 2: 4-10, Ephesians 3: 16-21, Philippians 4:19, I Thessalonians 4:13-18, I John 3: 1, 16, John 4:7-10, Revelation 21-22*

"TRUSTING ONLY JESUS ALWAYS!"
In Memory of the Reverend Luther Wright
Pastor C. Earl Mahan
Love of Christ Lutheran church
Weslaco, Texas
July 9, 2004

I learned yesterday of the death of my friend Luther Wright. How I learned of his passing was as strange and serendipitous as what I am learning from it. This shouldn't surprise me though. Nor should it surprise any of us who know Luther. He was always making us think about things and gently challenging us to reconsider deeply held assumptions. He was a teacher and a preacher in the very best sense these words have to offer. So, as I sit here less than twenty-four hours after learning of his death over the July 4th weekend just past, it comes as no surprise that as usual, with Luther class is still in session.

I learned of Luther's passing from a recorded message on the automated answering system at King of Kings Lutheran Church, in Lake Orion, Michigan. It was July 8th, and I had been intending and forgetting (putting off?) calling him for some time. We had played a short round of phone tag back in May. I was "it" and had let one thing after another keep me from returning the call. We had communicated by phone two or three times a year since I left Detroit in the mid 90's to return to my home state of Texas. Upon learning of his battle with a rare form of liver cancer, we had continued our occasional, though less frequent, phone conversations and each time we talked I became more and more aware of the shortness of time he had left. I am quite sure that my delays in calling him back had much more to do with my fears than with any excuses of being busy and simply forgetting to call.

"Enough already," I said to myself finally, "Pick up the phone and call him." As I was in my office, I didn't have his home phone number handy, so I looked up King of Kings from the ELCA website figuring I could call and get his home number from the office secretary. I got no answer at the church office, instead getting the office voice mail. It was then that I found out. After the initial greeting on the automated system, I heard, "For information about Pastor Luther Wright, press 106." My first thought was that with so many people like me calling for info, they had simply set up an informational update on the phone system to let people know of his health status. Instead what I heard was the information regarding the time and location of his funeral which had taken place the day before. I was mad at myself for having not called sooner to talk to my friend. I was mad at the cancer that had taken him from us too soon. I was mad at God for something that made no sense. Yet I know my anger was really just a front for my grief, for sadness over the loss of my friend and teacher. I grieve for his wife and children. I grieve for his congregation. I grieve for the church as a whole, for one of its finest minds and purest souls are no longer among us.

I have been thinking of Luther nonstop since learning of his death, shedding a few tears and wondering just what it was that made Luther such a special part of my life. I think more than anything he was a mentor to me, showing me how to be a pastor and how to do it with integrity, and all the while never taking oneself too seriously. He was not the only one of course. There have been many "men and women of the cloth" over the years that have taught me and shared with me their wisdom, but Luther was one of the most consistent. He was always ready to listen and give advice. He was always eager to share what new insights he was learning and putting into action in the congregations he served. He was always willing to name truth when he saw it, and likewise, to call the "bullshit" just that. No apologies. More than anything, he was utterly committed to proclaiming the gospel of our Lord Jesus Christ and letting nothing, and I mean nothing, get in the way of that task. Oh, if I had a dollar for every time he gave me that simple, yet profound admonition to, "Preach the gospel!" when I was feeling like giving up on everything and how those simple words would always put priorities back into focus for me!

I first met Luther the year I did my seminary internship. I was serving as intern at Christ Lutheran Church, in Detroit and Luther was pastor at Truth Lutheran Church. Christ and Truth were congregations belonging to the Detroit Lutheran Coalition, a handful of ELCA congregations doing ministry in that great city. Luther, along with a few other pastors I met that year, was committed to doing ministry in situations and places that most of us would not dream of. The "inner city" and all the connotations that come with that phrase was the context in which Luther and others were living out their calling to ministry. Not only that, these white pastors took very seriously the struggle for justice and the battle against the cultural realities of racism, classism, and sexism. As a student I learned the value in questioning why things are the way they are, even in the church. I learned the truth of my privileged status in society and in the church that came simply by virtue of factors that I had no control over whatsoever – my race, my class, and my gender. Conversely, I learned from this group of pastors, and the people we served, that these very same factors afforded others not privilege, but instead a life of injustice and inequality. Even more, I learned that because of the status afforded me by society, the nature of my call to the pastoral office demanded that I must always stand on the side of those not afforded such status, that no matter what context I was called in my life to serve as a pastor of the church, as a pastor of the church I had a responsibility to speak for justice on behalf of the oppressed.

My real learning from Luther began two years later, when upon completing seminary I returned to the Motor City to accept my first call as pastor of Olivet Lutheran Church. My closest neighbor in the Detroit Lutheran Coalition was Truth Church, where Luther served. We immediately began coming together, at first because of geography, but in time, out of what can only be called genuine brotherly love.

Luther took me under his wing. We met and talked every week, sometimes three or four times a week. We talked about how to deal with stubborn church councils and congregational members who resisted change. We talked about the challenge of being white clergy in black communities and black congregations, trying to pastor with integrity and humility. Luther had been a part of a group of Detroit pastors that had engaged in an ongoing process of intentional examination of issues related to this dynamic, with two African American Lutheran seminary professors, Dr. Rudy Featherstone of Trinity Lutheran Seminary and Dr. Pete Pero of the Lutheran School of Theology at Chicago.

I was able to glean insights from the wisdom Luther and the other pastors gained by going through such intentional study and struggle. Truth Church where Luther served was maybe a decade or two farther along in making that transition from white to black, not just in terms of who was sitting in the pews on Sunday morning, but how the congregation understood itself and let that identity shape it mission. I was able to learn from Luther from what he has been through in his first decade of ordained ministry, his successes and his failures. Most of all, with Luther's help and advice, I never felt alone.

I became a better preacher during those years. I had learned much about the art of homiletics, both in seminary and while on internship at Christ Church with Pastor Sue Ericsson, but it was with Luther that I first learned some of my most important lessons about the process of sermon creation. We called our time together "The Sermon Factory", time spent in Luther's office pouring over the scriptures and pouring out our souls. It was precious, holy time that I will not soon forget. It taught me the value and importance of being willing to open up and share with other fellow proclaimers of the gospel, to lay yourself and your ideas bare, with much prayer, sweat and tears.

I've never known a person who read the Word as much and as often as Luther. His Bible was the most marked up, highlighted, underlined, dog-eared, and scribbled in the margins thing you'd ever want to lay your eyes on. Its spine was covered in duct tape. He loved to find something in the Bible that he had never seen before, or a new way of looking at a text that he had never considered before. And when those ideas came, those "aha" moments where the pieces fell into place and the scripture was illuminated, he wasted no time taking it into the pulpit. His sermons were filled with energy and conviction and a pure desire to convey to others the ideas he was discovering in his study.

My time in Detroit, as I have mentioned, was short. After a little more than two years, I left Detroit to serve in San Antonio, Texas. It was hard for me to leave. I felt like I was giving up, throwing in the towel too soon. I felt the struggles I had encountered in my first call as a pastor in the inner city had gotten the better of me. I looked around at people like Luther and other pastors in the city who had stayed in equally, if not more difficult situations, but had managed to shepherd their flocks for long periods of time. I questioned my sense of call to the ministry. I felt like a failure. But Luther and others helped remind me of the grace that we preachers so often talk about, but so rarely let ourselves receive.

But Luther and others helped remind me of the grace that we preachers so often talk about, but so rarely let ourselves receive.

The thing that keeps us where we are, doing the work we do, for little pay and benefits, and even less appreciation, is that nagging "still, small voice" that whispered in our hearts long ago. Whether we were, like brother Luther, a long haired Florida surfer dude who heard the call on the waves of the Atlantic Ocean, or like myself, a kid from the suburbs of Houston who first heard the whisper as I served as an acolyte during my junior high confirmation years, or whatever it was we once were, the Lord Jesus called us by name and said, "Friend, have I got a deal for you...Come, follow me."

The last time I saw Luther was in 2000, in St. Louis, at the ELCA National Youth Gathering. It had been four years since we last saw each other, though we had talked on the phone every few months or so after I left Detroit to serve in San Antonio. We were both busy that week with our respective youth groups, but we both found time to meet one afternoon and let our groups take in the activities in the convention center, while we found a place to sit and talk.

Much had changed in both our lives. I was still serving in San Antonio at the time, but sensing that my time in that congregation was drawing to a close. Luther had left Detroit a year after I did to serve King of Kings Church, in Lake Orion, north of the city. The struggle to pastor in a place like Detroit had finally become too difficult for him. The toll that it exacts on one's spouse and children can be hard. More significantly though, he had heard that "still small voice" again, calling him to shepherd another flock of God's people. He had accepted that call and was, as usual throwing himself into his new congregation's mission and ministry with the same zeal and passion as he had in Detroit.

The move from city to suburb had changed things for him and his family. There was, to a certain degree, a greater sense of security that came with serving his new congregation. He had more resources and opportunities at his disposal. Yet many of the same old struggles were present, many of the same old personalities, which can paralyze a congregation into inaction where outreach and mission are concerned.

Luther faced it head on. He told me that day in St. Louis how he was applying the "Purpose Driven Church" (Rick Warren's book of the same name) principles to King of Kings, his new congregation, and how in just his first few years there he was helping them to transition to being a congregation where intentional discipleship formation is the number one priority. He had even managed to convince the congregation and the church council to actually suspend their constitution for a period of time while they looked at how new models and structures related to being a "purpose driven" congregation could be applied. If you are not Lutheran this might pass you by as being no big deal, but to anyone who has tried to work creatively within the narrow confines of your average Lutheran congregational constitution, along with all the aforementioned struggles the average pastor deals with on a daily basis, you know that to get a congregation to agree to suspend the constitution and essentially live with no solid framework while exploring new models for ministry is nothing short of miraculous. Luther, I'm sure, would have taken no credit for this, rightfully giving all honor and praise to the Lord, but to my mind it is a prime example of how Luther worked and what he was able to accomplish and lead others to accomplish. It's an example of one of those brief shining moments where a pastor and congregation are really on the same page and together are being used by God for the sake of God's kingdom. It in indicative of a slogan

I saw on the King of Kings website that I know has Luther's fingerprints all over it, "T.O.J.A. – Trusting Only Jesus Always!"

Later that day Luther talked me into joining him and some of the kids for a whiffle ball game there in the convention center. I was hesitant at first, but as usual Luther prevailed. There in the St. Louis convention center we two "old men" played the great American pastime with teenagers from our youth groups, as well as kids from all over the country. I don't remember how many games we won, but we were eventually eliminated by a bunch young kids that ran circles around us.

It reminded me of one summer in Detroit in which Luther talked several of us pastors into joining a softball league. Luther was our recruiter, manager, and coach. He had found the league, organized and scheduled practices, and even got us matching shirts and caps. We never won a game. He had mistakenly (?) signed our team up in the more advanced league, thinking we could hold our own. We couldn't. We didn't. We got trounced every game we played. We stunk really badly. That was for certain. But the guy on the pitcher's mound (guess who) never let us give up and never let defeat be anything other than an opportunity to try harder the next time.

"O God of grace and glory, we remember before you today our brother Pastor Luther Wright. We thank you for giving him to us to know and to love as a companion in our pilgrimage on earth. In your boundless compassion, console us who mourn. Give us your aid, so we may see in death the gate to eternal life, that we may continue our course on earth in confidence until, by your call, we are

reunited with those who have gone before us; through your son Jesus Christ our Lord. Amen" (Lutheran Book of Worship)

Pastor C. Earl Mahan

Chapter 17

Life Blood

"But now in Christ Jesus you who once were far away
have been brought near through the blood of Christ."
Ephesians 2:13

The next e-mail was Luther's last one written to a
large group. His purpose was to tell of Andrew Murray's:
<u>The Blood of Christ</u> and to share it with others because it
made quite an impression on him.

After he died, I gave the book to my dear friend Kim who
Luther had mentored for 15 years. Luther had shared with
her its power and had also made notes in it specifically for
her. She was able to share her views and the many blessings
that came from it.

It is at this point that things begin to go downward
for Luther. He was still receiving chemo but not without
pain and discomfort. The question of 'when is enough,
enough?' began to surface.

April 2, 2004

*Dear Sisters & Brothers in Christ and Co-workers as
Pastors and Evangelists,*
*   I pray that this email finds you weller than well in
body, soul, mind and spirit and that this is also true for*

your beloved ones.

I am pleased to brag up Our Father and testify: "If God is for us, who stands a chance to stand against us?! He who did not spare His own Son but gave him up for us all, will he not also give us all things with him? Of course!!!" Romans 8:32

Quick update: At the end of January I restarted my chemotherapy after my successful surgery in December. The clinical chemo plan is to have me undergo cycles once a week chemo for three weeks and then take a rest week. And then resume the next cycle, and to continue this regimen till death do us part. Nevertheless and yet I continue to pray for the miracle cure, the miracle remission, the miracle of outliving the clinical prognosis by the grace-full handiwork of our Father for whom nothing is too hard, too wonderful or too impossible for Him to do (let me be sure to add here that my quality of life remains excellent and does not match my clinical profile!). I am certainly in the latter of these three miracle categories (thanks be to God for answering the ceaseless prayers that you and the saints are offering up!), and though delighted to be in this category, I would welcome getting bumped up to miracle category two or one!

That being said, I must also share that from a clinical standpoint things are not going the way my oncologists would like. My tumor marker has reached an all-time high. Tumor markers indicate, in part, how aggressive the tumor is, and I've yet to be able to complete a three successive weeks of chemo. I get through with the second dose and then I come down with an infection. Yesterday I received the second dose in my third cycle. So please ask your prayer warriors to ask God to get me through this week and to and through dose three next week.

Now, to the book recommendation. When I went out on my mid-February shopping spree for Lent and Easter I looked for another of Andrew Murray's works. I'd been to the movies to see "The Passion of Christ" earlier in the week and so as I scanned the bookshelf looking for Andrew Murray books, lo and behold, what grabbed my eye was the red spine of a book titled <u>The Blood of Christ</u> by, you guessed it, one Andrew Murray! Now given that the graphic bloody images from "The Passion" continued to haunt my conscious and sub-conscious thinking I was both repelled and attracted to the book. I took it in my hands and read the billing on the back cover: "I am deeply convinced that we can never know too much about the truths the blood proclaims," Andrew Murray. I went on to read: Now together in one volume, Murray's 20 presentation set (10 in the Power of the Blood of Jesus and 10 in the Blood of Christ) take believers step-by step through Scripture to understand: 1) that there is no single scriptural idea, from Genesis to Revelation, more constantly and more prominently kept in view that that expressed by the word "the (sacrificial) blood", and 2) why the blood of Christ has unparalleled power and learn what promises were made to all believers when that blood was shed.

Murray's intent is to help Christians grasp the truth of redemption at the time of salvation and on through life as a follower of Christ. I must tell you that a chill ran up and down my spine, and goose bumps covered my flesh as I read this billing and had images of the movie flash through my mind. And then and there I was intrigued not only to purchase and read the book, but also to consider whether Mel Gibson as a denomination adherent to "fundamental Catholicism" was communicating something much more to the viewer with the gallons and gallons and gallons of blood than historical realism. But the many, many sins forgiven. Having completed the first 10 chapters in Murray's book, I think I can offer a definite YES to that question. I went and saw "The Passion" a second time, and my experience of the blood flow was much different as Murray's words played as sub-text to the sub-titles.

One final last nugget to share with you. This morning I started Part 2 of the book, the final 10 chapters. As I read the Preface to Part 2, I learned that Pastor Murray first presented these addresses to his South African congregation in the mid-1850s during Passion Week! As I looked at my calendar, at the rate of one chapter a day and by the grace of God, I will be taught by Murray during Passion Week 2004 and finish his 20th and final address on Easter Sunday! TOJA...Hah! Hah! Hah!

Enough said, eh?

Holy Week Meditation from Murray: "He who loved us and washed us from our sins in his own blood" Rev. 1:5... This love is indeed incomprehensible. What has His love not moved Him to do? He became sin for us: He was made a curse for us. Who would dare to use such language? Who could have ever thought up such a thing if God had not revealed it to us by His Spirit? That He really gave himself up for us, not because He was forced to do so, but only because of a love that longed for fellowship with us...that we might be forever identified with Him and him with us...is hard to comprehend.

Really now, enough said! Love to you and your beloved ones and your congregations.

Luther TOJA
Whose love for us is his blood for us; whose blood for us is his love for us!

My name is Kim Gibson and I was blessed to be one of many mentored by Luther. During his illness, when I went to visit him, Luther was always anxious to share his daily feast on God's word with me. I will never forget these times of being fed through the amazing wisdom God gave him.

His joy for the book, <u>The Blood of Christ</u>, was unequaled. Luther clearly understood the fullest meaning of the blood Jesus shed for us. On the side of the book he wrote "I am crucified with Christ" and "Christ lives in me" from Galations 2:20.

Through the shedding of His blood he covered our sins so we could be pure (white as snow), so He could enter our lives. The sacrificial blood is central through the whole Bible. When sin entered our lives in the Garden of Eden we were unfit, unholy to come into the presence and fellowship of God. The only way we could be secure in covering our sin came through substitution. The Israelites were passed over through substitution of the perfect lamb slain and its blood put over their doorway. The angel of death killed all the firstborn in the homes of those who had no sacrificial blood on the doorway. This blood saved their lives, but did not bring them into the presence of God. It was only through continuous sprinkling of the sacrificial blood. God Himself, the perfect lamb loves us so much...wants to have fellowship with us so much...wants us to reside with Him for eternity so much that He poured His own blood out for us to wash us clean of sin. What has His love not moved Him to do? It is not that we love Him, it is that He loved us. Without His blood there would be no relationship, no fellowship, no eternal life. He poured His blood out not because He was forced to but because of a love that longed for fellowship with us.

"And yet it is precisely this God, beyond my comprehension, the very God I can and must believe in, in faith, in hope, as no other! TOJA," a note from Luther in the margin of the book.

Chapter 18

Put on the Armor of God

"Finally, be strong in the Lord and His mighty power.
Put on the full armor of God so that you can take your
stand against the devil's schemes."
Ephesians 6:10-11

There were times during my journey with Luther
that I asked myself...Do I trust only Jesus? The truth:
sometimes I did not. I grew up a pastor's daughter and then
married a pastor. I had been in the church my whole life. To
admit I did not trust God was difficult. Sensing my troubled
heart, He showed me that I could, I must trust Him. In Him
all things are possible. On this side of Heaven we see only
a portion of the big picture. Life is a puzzle in which we
try to put the pieces where we think they should be and
at times they just don't fit. We get frustrated and give up.
This is ridiculous...we think. It's at this point that we must
outstretch our arms, fully opening and surrendering to God.
And when we get to the point of surrender, when we get
down on our knees and beg God to show us the way, He
takes us; mind, spirit, soul and heart and leads us down the
path he wants us to follow. He gives us calm and peace and
rest and guidance to help us with the grand puzzle that is
this life. It is at this point when we are wearing the armor of
God that we have the strength to endure. But even with the

armor on, there will be tough, troubled and sorrowful times. These times can be filled with the calmness of knowing God is guiding us and protecting us. How can we lose?

This next collection of writings began in May 2004 when Luther's cancer was growing faster and we knew in our hearts the battle would soon end. The sadness was heavy. The fear was paralyzing and our frustration level was elevated.

Yet, I found myself clinging tighter to God and knowing Him much more deeply. I discovered that feelings and emotions do not measure my faith. In my heart, I knew that even though I did not feel God, or trust God I knew He had not forsaken me and had not left my heart for one beating moment.

We have a great and wonderful God.

Updates from Sarah
May 2004

For the past two or so weeks Luther has been having trouble eating again. His last good meal was Mother's Day. We knew then. Today he had an upper GI done where he drinks barium and they watch to see where it goes. Unfortunately, what they saw was not good news. The area where the small intestine and stomach come together looks good but a little farther down the intestine is being closed off by the tumor. Whatever he does eat gets stopped at that point and eventually tries to force its way through the small area, which creates some of his bad pain. At this point he is drinking clear liquids to try and help the barium get through there. Monday he is scheduled for a CT scan which will hopefully show where the tumor is exactly so the doctor can decide what to do, if anything, next. Another reality day here in the Wright household. So for now he will get through the weekend with a few baseball games which lifts our spirits and then look to Monday to see what we are facing. So, of course, prayers are always welcome. I will continue to let you know what is happening.

Love, Sarah

May 25, 2004

Well, Luther went for his CT scan yesterday and after drinking 25oz of barium and sitting for a few hours, they began the scan only to realize the barium from the upper GI of last week was still in his intestine. They could not do the scan. Disappointing. We came home and he had several hours of pain due to the stuff trying to pass through a closed area. He is now only drinking liquids and will go to the oncologists' office today for IV hydration so that does not become an issue. The doctor's have rescheduled the CT scan for Friday. We will hopefully know more then. He now weighs 145 lbs but remains in pretty good spirits. He is getting tired of feeling pain whenever he puts anything in his stomach. He is very courageous and his humor keeps me laughing. I will keep you posted.

Love, Sarah

May 26, 2004

Last night Luther took a laxative to help in the process of ridding his body of the barium remaining from a previous test. About a half an hour later he was in serious pain, a 10 on the 10 point pain scale. There was no relief with the arsenal of meds and injections we have here. So when I told him I had spoken with the doc and his brother and both said he needed to go to the ER, expecting an argument, I got none and we left right away. We waited about two hours in the waiting room, which is quite maddening when he is in so much pain. As soon as they did get to him they gave him good IV pain meds which provided him with relief he had not felt in awhile. He was admitted to be hydrated and comfortable until a CT scan can be done and then we will go from there. A few things the doctor is looking at: 1) Is the tumor pressing on the outside of the intestine and pressing it closed? 2) Is the tumor wrapped around that area and closing it off or 3) Is the tumor penetrating the intestine and is causing the problem that way? Either way they are not sure what can be done. Hopefully by the weekend we might know something. So for now, he is pretty medicated. He has the same nurse he had awhile back. She lost a child three years ago and reminded him that he had told her he would pray for her. He told her he remembered and she said God must have answered some of those prayers because some of the things she was stuck on had been worked through. She then told him she continues to pray for him and awaits answers. How amazing, isn't it? God does send people into our lives everyday. Tonight he is resting and hopefully the pain will continue to be controlled and we will get answers soon. He did say he was not up to visitors at this point. But he would appreciate any prayers you might say on his behalf. I will keep you posted.

Love, Sarah

May 27, 2004

Our daughter, Amy turned 20 today. We celebrated her day at the hospital with Luther. Her boyfriend left for California this morning without even a card for her special day. Luther took this opportunity to express his deep concern about her relationship with someone who was not 'care-full' with her. He wanted her to be with someone who treated her with the love and respect she deserved. His expression of father-love for her was tender and quite honest. He taught the kids 'know your worth, honor your worth and value your worth.' Listening to him as a dad, knowing he wouldn't be with us much longer, was very moving. There was an urgency in his words.

The kids and I then went to dinner, at Luther's request, which has always been our tradition and got a taste of what our lives were going to be like when he was gone. It was a bittersweet day.

May 29, 2004

I do not have any new news yet but wanted to check in. Luther is having better luck with pain, maybe at a four or five on the 10 point scale. He was pretty heavily medicated today and did not like how he felt. Out of sorts is how he describes it. Tonight they have tried to move the barium along. He is frustrated because they keep insisting he drink large amounts of things to help things move, but it appears they do not understand that: "IT DOES NOT GO THROUGH!!!!!" So we will see. In the waiting area with Don and Carol Ann, Luther was to drink 20 oz of a laxative that tasted like seaweed. One sip and he looked at us and said, "NOPE". He told the nurse he was sorry but he was not going to drink it. She did not argue with him.

They are hoping to do the CT scan tomorrow. Hopefully that will happen successfully. I got home about 11:30 pm and spent some time out on my patio on my swing. I enjoyed the peacefulness and being reminded that my God is here with us and watching very closely. I feel so grateful for that. For tonight I know He is with my Luther holding him and loving him. Now I can go to bed trusting Luther is being held closely. Good night.

Love, Sarah

May 30, 2004

No CT scan yet. They are still trying to clear things from the upper GI. They will x-ray this morning and hopefully be able to do it today. Yesterday afternoon Luther spiked a temp of 102.6. Not good. Blood work, ice packs under the armpits, and it came down to 101.4 which is where it is today. This is a sign of infection in the liver or the stent in his bile duct or a blockage in the stent which is not what we want to have happen.

He is on antibiotics and they are watching him closely. Unfortunately, he is beginning to itch, which happens when there is an infection or blockage in the liver. And so far there is no good solution for relief from the itching other than Benedryl IV which knocks him out. So for today pray for comfort and the antibiotic to do their magic and the itching to be relieved.

<u>Streams in the Desert</u> May 21: The other day my bible study time was talking about the fabled nightingale bird never sings while his cage is full of light but when darkness comes, his melody is so sweet. It is extremely doubtful if a soul can really know the love of God in its fullness and in its comforting until the skies are black and dark. Light comes out of darkness and morning out of the dark of night...

As I read this out on my swing it rang true for me. Even in my deepest darkness and fears, God is true. The darkness...Cancer is darkness...But Your light shines... Pain is darkness...But Your love abounds...Sadness is darkness...But Your loving arms are everlasting... Death seems dark...Yet You ARE the victory. The one who saves us from the darkness. Darkness on Good Friday upon the cross, is light, glorious light on Easter morning. HE IS ALIVE!! He is risen indeed. Amen. So on this Sunday morning I will look for His light and love throughout the day and I will call out to Him and He will hear me. Thank you all for your love and prayers.

Love, Sarah

May 30, 2004

Sunday night and Luther is still not home. They were able to do the CT scan, but our doctor's partner was on call this weekend and really had no information for us. It appeared he was not up to date on Luther's case, which is frustrating when things seem to be progressing for Luther. He needs to be 24 hours without a temp before he can come home. He is now jaundiced and still itching, but it seems the bile count is going down which means infection in his liver and not a stent blockage. At this point it is good in the sense that if the stent blocks there is no way to get it out and things get complicated. So more blood work in the morning to make sure things are going in the direction they should. Hopefully home tomorrow. We are scheduled to see Luther's doctor on Wednesday at his office so maybe more info then. I guess for now this is one of those days when trusting Jesus only is all we can do. Talk to you tomorrow.

Love, Sarah

May 31, 2004

He is home! There was no way he was staying one more day. At noon, there we sat, still waiting. Luther went to the nurse's station and asked to have the doctor paged. He was told they do not do that for patients. Luther said, "He told me I would be discharged by noon and I am still here. Please page him." They did. I guess they knew he would not take no for an answer. Ten minutes later in walks the doctor. It was a frustrating *hospital stay because his doctor was out of town and it was a holiday weekend. This was the first time Luther was 'non-compliant' during this whole process. He wanted to get home! Because it was a holiday weekend, they were short staffed and he was told to wait patiently for a wheelchair. There were three others in front of him to be discharged. He sat there for about 15 seconds and decided he wasn't waiting. He started for the elevators and was stopped by an aide who said he could not leave without an orderly. He said… "So sue me." I was waiting out in the van and when I saw him walking out I knew what had probably happened. A man counting minutes in his life and he was going to spend every last one of them with his family, not waiting on a wheelchair. But he is home and we are very happy. We see his doctor on Wednesday and maybe talk about what is next if anything. Thanks for your prayers and love. Sarah*

Chapter 19

It was by Faith

"The fundamental fact of existence is that this
trust in God, this faith, is the firm foundation under
everything that makes life worth living. It's our
handle on what we can't see."
Hebrews 11:1 MSG

When going through struggles in this life it always seems there is a time when reality stares you straight in the face and denial can no longer be an option.

As we attempted daily to remain faithful and focused on Jesus, the harsh reality of pain, sorrow, end-of-the-road decisions seemed to continually blind us. I knew deep in my heart that this part of our journey would some day come, but hoped it would be longer down the road or perhaps one of those miracles you hear about would happen to us. It was not to be.

The agonizing, heavy heart and soulful pain I felt while watching my husband come closer and closer to death was a painstaking burden. Sometimes I felt like giving up. I thought my heart would break into millions of pieces just watching, waiting, enduring. What do you pray for at such a time? Healing? Pain relief? Cancer to disappear? Death? I was torn inside. The weight was heavy. However, in the midst of despair, God was there. He gave us both resilient determination for a little more of life together here on this earth.

Ben's baseball games were a tremendous highlight and goal. There was joy in watching him play. The love we felt from parents, players and friends was a gift. It carried us and revived us through this part of the race.

These next writings describe Luther's final hospital stay and our awareness of the final days to come. As the unbearable lay ahead of us, God made certain to lift the load and carry us through-oh what a comfort God's arms provided.

Updates from Sarah
June 1, 2004

Well, Luther was home for a short time. Today about 5 a.m. began serious pain. It continued several hours and once again I was not able to get it under control with the meds here. I called his oncologist and she suggested going to the ER. I told her he was in too much pain to go and sit and wait for a couple of hours. She said for me to call an ambulance and she would call ahead to the ER. I called the ambulance and within 1-2 minutes they were here. Amazing!!!! We got to the ER and they were waiting for us. They took him to a room and by the time I got him registered they had him hooked up to IV pain meds. Luther lay there quiet, finally the pain relieved. There were five of us there reading Luther's favorite psalms out loud. We all had a calm feeling. Luther asked Kim, my closest friend, to lean in closely. She went to him and he said, "don't go anywhere near the ball field." We roared with laughter. Ben had a game later that day and it seemed whenever Kim went to a game, they lost.

He was there for about two hours when they took him to his room, which was a private room. We thought 'how did we get so lucky?' We later found out the oncologist had called and made that arrangement. He is there now until the gastroenterologist and oncologist can put their heads together. For now he is much better on the pain meds and will not come home until the IV meds can be set up at home or a correction of the intestinal problem. We will see what is in store for him now. As tough as the day was, there were many blessings showered on us and I feel very grateful. God's hands are always a work.

Love, Sarah

June 3, 2004

Dear friends and family,

Well this is the email that I was hoping not to have to write, but it is at the point where we have come. Yesterday we were able to speak with all four of Luther's doctors and they were all in agreement that we have come to the end of the road in terms of trying things to stop the tumor growth. It seems the cancer has infiltrated the large and small intestine along with other changes in his abdomen that suggest the cancer has also spread elsewhere. It was a kind of relief that they all said the same thing because now we know we have gone down every possible road of earthly healing. Needless to say we feel great sadness at what lies ahead. Luther will come home today with Hospice in place for pain control. We are also hoping for IV hydration because he is unable to get any nutrition by mouth. Hospice is working quickly to get things in order to get him home. Our goal is to get him home and comfortable enough to get to Ben's playoff games tomorrow. I ask for prayers for strength and the right meds so that will take place. God knows our hearts so well I am sure what ever is best will happen. As I sit here this morning it is all too real to me and I want him home NOW! We have had time to talk with the kids and immediate family and I know we all feel the same heavy heart. As I look at him, I still find myself in disbelief that this is our next step. I certainly have to trust that God is present and in control, for what else do we have? I feel grateful for each and every day.

We know that people want to able to see him and say good-bye and we want to honor that. We are trying to think what would be the best for him and we will let you know when we have worked out a plan.

Prayers for today…Luther: that his amazing faith will keep him strong and close to our mighty God who will protect and care for him in these last remaining days… Amy and Ben: that God's tender mercy will watch over and touch them and reassure them of His great love and that they can Trust Him always… Sarah: for strength and courage and love to care for Luther each minute of each day…Luther's mom: pray that she is surrounded by God's love and love of all around her, keep her close, Lord…Luther's family…God's tenderness, comfort, mercy, strength.

For now, my love to you all, remembering in these difficult times especially that we need to trust only Jesus *always, now more than ever.*

Love , Sarah

The following day I went to the hospital to bring Luther home, but there was a problem. The Hospice we called would not provide IV hydration at home. Dr. Amnuay took charge. He cancelled those plans and called the visiting nurse association. It was nice to know we had such loving physicians, willing to go the extra mile, miles for us. With this change in plans, Luther had to wait another day to come home.

It was important for all of us to get Luther home and to Ben's baseball games the following day. He told me not to set myself up for disappointment because timing may not allow that to happen. Little did my husband know of my inner determination to succeed. God and I WILL get him home the next day AND God and I WILL get him to the games. I PROMISE!

June 4, 2004

Luther came home this morning. I cut his hair and he took a shower, much to his delight. The hospital bed came and my brother Steve and family arrived and off we went to the game. Wonderful!!!! When we got there the team greeted us at the gate and all of the boys came over and greeted Luther one by one. Wonderful!!!!! Ben played left field and had a terrific game. They won the first game 2 – 1. The District Championship game started about 45 minutes later and Luther was doing great. The pain was controlled and people were thrilled to see him. The 2nd game we won 7-1, which makes the team District Champs!!! Next weekend is regional playoffs, so now we look forward to that. Luther came home and took a shower and has been dozing. It has been a very full day for a man who was in the hospital for nine days. He is driven.

Tomorrow the visiting nurse comes and starts the IV fluids and will teach me how to connect and disconnect the IV. The nurse will always do the needle in his port, but can teach me the other stuff. Luther's oncologists are amazing people and watch closely over him. I like that. He will get IV fluids eight hours per day and also get IV pain meds if needed.

Today was very fabulous and glorious. I feel very grateful.

Love, Sarah

Personal Letter
Dr. Amnuay Singhakowinta, MD
Luther's oncologist

Dear Sarah,

Cancer of the bile duct is a very rare type of malignancy in this country. There are less than 4,000 new cases per year in the U.S. (as opposed to more than 200,000 per year for breast cancer). The only known effective treatment is surgical resection, if cancer can be detected early. However, it is quite rare that the cancer is diagnosed early enough. The five years survival at the present time is only 10 – 15% despite treatment (almost *entirely by partial resection of the involved portion of the liver and bile duct).*

For a little more advanced disease, when both lobes of the liver are involved but the cancer is still confined to the liver, the liver transplant from a related donor is an attractive approach. Whether or not it is the way to go, is hard to say due to the small number of candidates and the difficulty in finding the donor. Radiation therapy has been disappointing. Likewise available chemotherapy has not done a very good job either. The only hope we have is to continue to explore the new drugs. But, because of rarity of this type of cancer, our chance of coming up with new drugs is going to take a much longer time than other common cancers like the breast, prostate and lung.

Reverend Wright was a pleasant and unique patient. He was the man who was always in charge. He was fully aware of the seriousness of the situation and yet he was trying to lift the spirits of all of us who were involved his care. He was more concerned about other people's feelings and well being than his own. He was the "dream" patient that any doctor wants to care for. He listened, took the advice and carried out the recommendations to the best of his ability and yet he showed us in a polite way who was the boss. It was the highest honor and a great privilege for me to be chosen and trusted to care for him until the end. He did finish his duty on earth faster than most of us and now in the better place, is praying for us all.

Chapter 20

Eternal Promises

"For God so loved the world that he gave his one and only Son, that whoever believes in him shall not perish but have eternal life." John 3:16

I have read the Resurrection Story over and over. I am filled with both joy and gratitude because of what Jesus did for us. He died a terrible death on Good Friday, and rose again on Easter. We can look forward to the same eternal promise.

These next writings remind me that God is love and He will be faithful to us. As Luther's confusion increased, he struggled to overcome it by trying to figure out the medications and how much he was getting at any given moment. As his life came to an end, his heart was filled with not only love for Amy, Ben and me, but also for Jesus who keeps His eternal promises.

Updates from Sarah
June 11, 2004

As this process continues, I am amazed how God keeps on working and sending wonderful people into our lives. I have found myself looking forward to the next day to see what God is up to.

Things are getting to a tough point. Luther is becoming more confused. As soon as his eyes close for sleep, it strikes. His concern is that he will become agitated while confused and be too much for me to handle alone. He asked the kids to stay close by to help me. Fluid that the tumor produces is now filling up his abdomen. It causes much pain and discomfort. He is not able to drink anything except to take pills. It only inflates his stomach, which also causes much pain. All of the drugs and things here are hard to control it. We had a nurse coming in to do IV fluids because the Hospice we had contacted does not do IV hydration. WELL… then today came. We decided to try a different hospice. They came out today and agreed to do the hydration AND now he is on an IV pain pump!!!! Amazing!!!! He was hooked up for 15 minutes and his pain was down to a three from a seven. The two nurses that were here today were wonderful. Angels, I do believe. One of the amazing things, too, was that this morning I was hooking up Luther's IV and stood up and felt every muscle in my back knot up. Quite painful. I thought "I can't do this." My neighbor, who is a massage therapist, came over and tried to make it better. As the nurse was hooking up the pain pump, I realized, all of a sudden, my back was better. I think the tension release from knowing his pain was going to be controlled was much more than I could have thought. Amazing what stress will do to the body. I think I also learned that I do not have to do all of this by myself and need to call on others to help. After all, what are friends for?

So for now we live day to day and love our time together. Monday, June 14 is our 24th Anniversary. A great day to celebrate.

Love, Sarah

June 16, 2004

    Just a quick note to keep you up to date, our 24th anniversary was special. Luther had a lot of pain that day which started the day out tough, but the Hospice nurse happened to call to see if we needed anything. She came, called the doc, calculated the IV pain pump and with a 500% increase was able to get the pain to a measure where by evening we were able to have some family "Jesus" time and it was very nice. God continues to work those miracles everyday. Earlier that afternoon, a few of Ben's friends were over. Luther, with his IV pole, staring out the window, turned and said, "Well boys, Daddy's stoned." The boys were rolling with laughter. He then asked if it was alright to go to God's Word stoned? The answer...absolutely!

    Margaret, a harpist friend of ours came over to play her harp for awhile. The music was from Heaven. It was gentle, soothing and just what we needed.

    The next day he felt good enough to go out in our friend's boat. How amazing!!!!! Today was quite busy with equipment being delivered, Hospice people visiting and other calls and visits. This evening we were able to have some quiet time, just Luther and I, also very nice. He started to spike a temp last night, so we are trying to get that under control. At this point he is pretty yellow with the infection in his liver, or the stent plugged or liver breakdown. It is hard to tell. He remains very uplifted by what Jesus continues to do and amaze us with. We feel completely surrounded by God's love and grace and mercy. He is truly our keeper. I keep telling people that we seem to live minute to minute. For tonight all is well. God is here and we are together. What more could we ask for?

Love, Sarah

June 24, 2004

Luther's prayer today was this… "You Father, reveal to us as husband and wife when it will be time to say, 'enough is enough.' It is finished. Into thy hands I commit my spirit."

This was the last day he was able to do his Bible time on his own. His body was jerking from the heavy doses of medication and continued confusion didn't allow him to do it anymore. I began reading out loud to him the Streams in the Desert *and the Bible. It was gift for us both.*

June 25, 2004

Today was his last day of conscious, clear thinking. The Hospice nurse needed to get him off of the heavy dilaudid and on to other meds that would knock him out. He asked her to wait 24 hours to do this. He called family and told them to come. It was such a strange time. To get to the point where you know you only have a few more hours to hear him talk and to feel his touch.

He said his good-byes to me that night. Our hearts

were completely open and our emotions raw with love and honesty. As we were talking and still trying to believe this was our life story, he told me as he has thought about it, all he could figure was God allowed this to be our path, he dying of cancer at such a young age, because He wanted me to be a blessing in someone else's life. For him, knowing we had gotten to the "enough is enough" point and to be so honest, I will treasure it always.

June 26, 2004

Let me begin by saying love is abounding here. A miracle is now happening at the Mayo Clinic for George who has the same cancer as Luther, but is still in the running for a transplant. I opened my email at 1:15 a.m. to read that he is in surgery right now getting the transplant. Praise God! I just knew that George would receive new life here on this earth just as Luther will receive new life with Jesus. Tonight it is time to begin praying for peace and comfort for Luther and all who love him and that God be merciful and take him to be with Him soon. Over the last two weeks things have changed quickly and in the last 48 hours other great changes. He is confused partly by the amount of medication, but mostly because of the toxins the liver is producing. He is struggling to be clear of mind and his body is not doing what he wants it to. We had some very wonderful time together today while the kids were out for awhile. God gave him enough clarity to tell me of his great love for me and for us to say our special good byes. I will cherish that time forever. I am sad to say that his battle is nearly over. He has put up a tremendous fight and lived well, laughed often and loved much. I am grateful to have been such a part of his life and he of mine. I am truly comforted by the knowledge that the same arms of God that will hold my sweet Luther are the same arms that hold and sustain Amy, Ben and me. The same God, same arms, same love holding us. Very nice. It is a very sad day indeed and yet a joyful day in the lives of George and Carla. God, what a nice touch. Thank you.

My love to you all, Sarah

June 26, 2004

Today started with heavy confusion… this brilliant man… heart crushing to see. His body was out of control with jerking movements. The family was here. The house was filling up with much love. There were people calling, visiting, and God's provision was as great as when Jesus walked this earth. Ben and Amy's friends kept constant watch over them. I will never forget the love shown to them during this time. I certainly know how difficult it must have been for kids at their ages to do this. But they did it and with great love and tenderness.

That night with all of us worn from watching Luther's body and mind rebel, a nurse, Michelle, came at 11:00 p.m., an angel of God, I am certain. We were all in the room with her as she cared for Luther and injected valium into his IV. Miracle. Within 15 minutes his body had calmed, no more jerking. Quiet, peaceful relief. We all felt the blessing of her care, tenderness and gentleness. Luther was finally calm. This was the beginning of the coma.

For the next hours and days we sang to him, prayed with and for him and read the Bible to him. We talked in the room like he was part of the conversation. There was love, laugher, crying, touching and caring for him. Love continued to build in our room and our house. God's great love. Family love. Friend's love. King of King's love. My Mom once said, "I have placed Luther and you and Amy and Ben in God's arms. You are safe there." That is exactly where we were. Safe in God's arms and it felt glorious.

I believe if Luther could tell us one thing it would be of God's GREAT love for us and for us to completely surrender our lives to Him because our God is in control. He is in charge. We need not worry. We can put our trust in Him. He is faithful.

Chapter 21

Happy Father's Day

"Yet this I call to mind and therefore I have hope:
Because of the LORD's great love, we are not
consumed, for his compassions never fail.
They are new every morning;
Great is your faithfulness."
Lamentations 3:21-23

This letter is from Ben to his dad on Father's Day 2004. Ben read it to him on that special day and also read it at Luther's funeral. When he was done reading, the congregation began applauding and gave him a standing ovation.

On this very special Father's day I decided that I was going to write you a letter. Over these past 17 years of you being my father, I am proud to say that we haven't had a large fight that I can remember. We have had fights due to sports, when you played quarterback for us (which no other Dad did) and I would lose, and I, being the poor sport I was, took it out on you. Little did I know, and I just expected dads to play with their sons, not many other dads do that. No other dads miss work for the kids, to coach, for dinner, and to make family first. You always apologize and say how you feel bad for the first years in Lake Orion when you had to work a lot. The thing is...you never missed anything! And the fact of the matter is that you made one church (at the time one church with two different types of people) into a very faith-driven church. I always took for granted the things you did with church, and how you preached, and how you treated people. I thought every pastor did this with their congregation. They don't. King of Kings Lutheran church is a very successful church led by faith. Everything you do is very genuine and I have realized this my whole life. Without your leadership, there wouldn't be a need to be building on at the church. I didn't know at the time, but your sermons are very interesting if you listen (sometimes I have trouble with that as you know). I have listened to other pastors, and you have a way of connecting peoples' lives to the Bible. You are the best pastor I have ever had!

As a husband you are extraordinary! I have never witnessed an argument between you and Mom. I am aware that no other kid can say that about their parents. You show so much love toward Mom and I hope that I can do that with my wife. When I get married I am going to try and follow your and Mom's footsteps because you guys live the perfect marriage. Like you said in one of our family talks, you have lived the happiest marriage you could have thought possible. You are one flesh indeed. When it is a holiday or an anniversary, you are so creative that it is nearly impossible to think what you will do next. The way your mind works is just so amazing that I can't believe the things you do. The CD's we made are just flat out remarkable and how you can remember all of the songs you guys had together. You have always put Mom first in every situation, and whenever you need to make a decision you bring it to Mom first. You guys set the perfect way to look and live out your marriage.

As my father, I am speechless. All of the things you do for me and Amy I wouldn't ever expect, but that is just the type of man you are. You never settle for the norm. You always go the extra distance for Amy and me. You have been completely open with her and me, and you always include us on what is going on. I am just going to list all of the things you and I have done together, that NO other father and son do on a regular basis: you coached ALL of my teams growing up. I played in 63 baseball games (two years of which you were battling cancer) and you missed only three games. You taught me how to play and love every sport I do (especially baseball; you passed the love of the game down to me). You played catch with me whenever I wanted even if you didn't have time-you made time. You quarterbacked over 1,000 games in the backyard, you always made time to be home for dinner, you have never missed a school event, you went on field trips, went to the Big Red Machine reunion baseball game for the Cincinnati Red's, you took me to a camp in Ohio. We created games to play outside on the basketball court, you painted the driveway for basketball lines (most dads would say no), you trust me (which is tough for some teenager's dads). I can honestly say that I have kept no secrets from you. You are truly my best friend. You build a tree fort in the woods, created very good relationships with all of my friends, and so many others, but the most important one you have showed me, is the way to live your life by faith. I know that I haven't done it yet, but some day I will come around to it. I will open up all of those books you have given me. You are a true example of how to live your life through God, and it makes me see how much God does in our lives.

I remember when Grandpa passed away, and it was just me and you looking over him. You hugged me and said "Benjamin, I hope that I can be half of the father he was to me, to you". And that you have. There is nothing that you and I don't have that I would want. I don't know of any other father and son that have the relationship that you and I have. When I finally grow up I hope that I can make a difference in half of the people you have, I hope I can be half the man you are. My baseball coach said you can tell what kind of a person a man was by how many people are at his funeral… look around. I hope that I live my life on the example you have set for Amy and I to follow. I have cherished every single moment with you, and that we continue to have. I honestly have been the luckiest son in the world. You are the "Miracle Man". I truly am the happiest son. There is not one thing I would have ever changed in our relationship you and I have built. And when I have kids, there are always going to hear about Luther Wright, because I am going to try and live my life the right way, and that's through God. I LOVE YOU SO MUCH!!! AND I WOULD NEVER TRADE ANYTHING THAT WE HAVE SHARED TOGETHER!!!! I hope this is the greatest Father's Day you have ever had, because it will be the most memorable one to me. I just want to thank you for everything you have done for Mom, Amy and me. You have been the greatest husband, father, and teacher. People always say you are "different and weird" (they mean it in a good way of course). You are different, weird, and unique, because there is no one else like you in the world! I just hope I can come close to that. The biggest compliment I have ever been given was by a person from church, I can't remember who, in fact a lot of people have said it, they say "You know Ben, you have so many traits of your Dad," and every time I hear that I smile, because that is the biggest compliment I can ever receive. I love you so much. You're my father and my best friend! And I am the luckiest son on this earth!

Love you, Ben

Chapter 22

House of Love

"For I am convinced that neither death nor life,
neither angels nor demons, neither the present
nor the future, nor any powers, neither height nor
depth, nor anything else in all creation, will be able
to separate us from the love of God that is in Christ
Jesus our Lord." Romans 8:38-39

In Romans 8 we are reminded nothing can separate us from the love of God. Not death. Not Satan. God's love for us is the victor. Although Satan may try to stir things up and add confusion and chaos to the mix of life our God reigns. What comes from the stirring and chaos and trials of life is a closer relationship with Christ. Oh how Satan must hate being a loser. Trust Jesus, the one who bled and died for you. Jesus is Risen! He is Risen indeed.

As Luther continues to hang on, (he has always been a stubborn fighter), we continue our loving vigil. Sometimes I would wonder if he wanted to die alone with no one in the room with him. At times, I would leave the room and tell him if he wanted that, I would give him five minutes, alone. But then I would be back. Not much time, I know, but I wanted to leave it to him.

While in the coma, we carried on as if he were a part of things, talking openly, reading out loud, laughing, crying, not really sure how much of it he could hear or understand.

The Holy Spirit filled and surrounded our house with so much love and peace that whoever entered experienced God's amazing love. Love was all around.

The two times he woke during that week, he knew exactly what was happening. He woke the first time to tell me he loved me and this second time… "The Kiss". My most memorable moment. Oh the love and joy in my heart and my sweet Luther's. I truly was blessed to share my life with him. We always believed God brought us together. God truly blessed us.

June 28, 2004

Luther continues to hang on. He is such a fighter. Yesterday at 4:45am we thought death would come at any minute. He was struggling to breathe due to the "terminal congestion". David, with his physician's wisdom asked for a turkey baster. Not having one we called a church/neighbor at this early hour, went to their house and got their baster. Don, Luther's brother, in his engineer's wisdom found a straw and requested the gum Kim was chewing. He and David constructed a suction devise clearing the congestion. Such brotherly love is this. Luther now rested comfortably. We are all amazed.

Luther is not responsive but does have a moment or two where we are sure he knows we are there. In his brief moment of awareness he was able to tell me he loved me. I'll never forget it. Very touching.
Sunday morning I was saying to my sister-in-law, Carol Ann, I know people at King of Kings want to do something and it would be cool to have them come and

surround the house and pray. Thirty minutes later a friend came over and said people would begin coming to the house at 2:00 p.m.. I asked her why they were coming and she said people were coming to encircle the house and pray. I looked at my sister-in-law and asked if she had said something to someone at church about my thought and she said, "No." Spirit lead. I just started laughing out loud at the wonderment of God in all of this. The prayer gathering at the house yesterday was about as Holy Spirit directed as it gets. For you see, at the very moment I was saying I know people want to do something, our friend, Dave, was at church saying, "It would be nice to do something." God knows our needs and provides. There were 150 people here surrounding our entire house singing, praying, and praising God with hands lifted to Jesus.

So for now, we continue to hold vigil over Luther, praying and singing and reading his favorite Bible verses and stories. I know he hears and is comforted.

Love, Sarah

July 2, 2004
"The Kiss"

We continue our minute to minute vigil with Luther. David, as a physician is amazed at what continues to sustain Luther. It must be love. We now have two sanctuaries in this house. One is my swing and sunflowers on the porch and the other is our bedroom where the Holy Spirit is active and alive and always amazing us with His presence. Just when we feel weary and think we can't continue the vigil again thru the night, someone or something happens that shows us that God's timing is perfect and we again become revived and joyful as we continue to sing, pray, and read from the Bible. At this rate we may get the whole thing read, which is perhaps what Luther intended. He continues in a coma that he has been in since Sunday. His last fluid was at seven p.m. a week ago today. He always said he wanted to get to July 4th because that is the day he found out about the cancer two years ago. Perhaps this is the last line he will draw and cross over. We have been sure to let him know this is now July. So we wait and wonder and cry and talk and love him tenderly. Then yesterday! David, Don and I had just finished bathing him and putting on new sheets when they stayed in the room for me to get some dinner. David came rushing into the kitchen and said "guess who is waking up and you need to get in there". Of course we all go running and there he was trying to open his eyes and trying to speak. His mouth and tongue were very dry and he was not able to form words. I was kissing his cheek and forehead when my nieces said give him a kiss on the lips. I did and he closed his lips enough to let me know he was kissing me. Wow! I look over to my nieces as if to say "did that really happen?" They were crying tears of joy so I figured it was real. I then told him I thought that was the sweetest kiss I have ever gotten. Then I said, "Well, I think our first kiss was pretty sweet too," and he crinkled up his forehead as if to say Yes, it was. I have been floating ever since. He was able to blink his eyes a few more times for about 10 minutes and then went back into the coma. A true gift from my God. All of these things happen to prepare us for the day when Luther does go to Jesus. We feel so lifted up in this house. Laughter fills the house and it is so wonderful to relive memories. I never imagined it being like this. I know sadness is there, but the joy, the joy, ah the joy is there, too. God sees our every need and provides. People bringing food is like the feeding of the 5,000, always more than enough. We feel your love and thoughts and they too sustain us. Someone asked me how many people we have here and I really don't know. The number changes daily. I spend so much time in the bedroom with Luther while things elsewhere in the house of love get done. Another God provision. So many provisions, I am sure I miss some of them. All I know is this is holy ground here and God is holding Luther and all of us and you so tenderly and lovingly. What joy fills my heart!

Our friend, George, after his liver transplant, is doing great. He is hoping to leave the hospital tomorrow. Isn't that something? Luther and George on their journeys, all guided and controlled by God. Who would have thought?

I will keep you posted and up to date about Luther. He continues to be an amazing man. I feel very blessed to have spent as much of my life with him as I have.

Love, Sarah

This sermon was written by my brother, Pastor Steve Bauerle on Luther's last Easter. I know He and Luther had spoken prior to Easter about a sermon but did not know the gist of it. Steve e-mailed it to me on July 1, 2004 and I thought that would be what I read to Luther that evening. As I began to read it what joy came over me. Luther's love for Amy, Ben and me is so great, so deep. It fills me with joy and tenderness, but also sorrow. How we will miss him in our lives. And yet, his message of hope in Jesus to us was and is tremendous, as always. After all, that was always Luther's message. Jesus died and rose again for you and for me so we could live with Him forever.

Dear Family and Friends,

I preached this sermon at Zion, Waterville on Easter 2004, with much of Luther's input. I asked him, "What would you say to my people on your LAST Easter?" He asked me to write it out and send it to Sarah, Amy and Ben. I have also included YOU. So, here it is.

Love, Steve

Easter Sermon, 2004
Preached by Pastor Steve Bauerle
"Edited" by Pastor Luther Wright
John 20: 1-18

THERE IS MORE TO THE STORY

Three days ago, on Good Friday, in this very sanctuary, death made his presence. Along with death, people from our church portrayed sorrow, agony, fear, shame and hate, all who were there 2,000 years ago at the cross on Good Friday. In between each portrayal, we sang a verse to the song WERE YOU THERE. Each character told the story of how they were at the cross of Jesus...but failed to overcome him. Death was the last character that appeared. He was dressed in all black. Black cape. Black gloves. Black veil. He began his portrayal by standing there mocking and laughing AT us, not with us. He said to us, "I was there, and, unlike my colleagues, I did not fail. Sooner or later every man falls beneath my power, and this man, Jesus was no different from the rest. He made lots of promises. He called himself the resurrection and the life. But today I proved that even he must submit to my eternal darkness. Tonight I reign victorious. Tonight I proved that the peace, joy and love that he spoke of, melt away in my presence. I am death, and the victory is mine!" When he was finished, he laughed and mocked his way out of our sanctuary. Ha Ha Ha Ha! Then, there was total silence in our sanctuary. You could have heard a pin drop. Children were clinging to their parents. Adults were sitting in awe. We were clearly reminded that death did have his day with Jesus and he will have his day with us. Yet, as he walked past me, you don't know how much I wanted to stand up and say to him, "Death, there is more to the story. You are not telling it all."

As we come together this morning, this Easter Morning, 2004, you notice who is laughing and celebrating now. You and me! Not death. For today we celebrate and live in the hope of Jesus' resurrection of the dead. It gives us hope in our lives that we too shall rise from the dead and Jesus did this for us not only for our own resurrection but he did it so we can have a personal relationship with him changing our lives forever. And we can shout, HE IS RISEN, HE IS RISEN INDEED. HALLELUAH!

Someone once asked me, "What defense do I have against other religions and people who oppose or hate Christians?" He went on to say that many religions have inspiring teachers, live by strong morals, perform miracles, and lead a good life. What defense do I have?" My answer to him was, "The resurrection." There is no other religion in the world that can proclaim that they have a personal savior who rose from the dead so that you can!

If you have not seen Mel Gibson's movie THE PASSION, I highly recommend it to you because of once scene. The one scene had nothing to do with the sophisticated means of torture that they did to Jesus using devises and whips. The one scene that I recommend to you in the movie has nothing to do with the mob mentality or the so-called trial that took place. The one scene did not have anything to do with what happened on that Friday, some 2,000 years ago. It was not the view from outside the empty tomb looking in with the linen cloths waving in the wind. The scene that I recommend to you, was the very last, where they showed a close-up picture of Jesus, so pure and clean, alive and well, risen from the dead for you and me.

As many of you know, my brother-in-law, Pastor Luther Wright is dying of liver cancer. Not only is he my brother, but he has become a mentor, a colleague and a friend as well. I have updated you over the last year and half on his condition. Once in a while, on a special occasion here at Zion, I say to him, "If you were preaching to them on this special occasion, what would you say?" Last year on Stewardship awareness Sunday, I e-mailed him and said, "In thirty words or less, what do you tell them on this day." After a number of days I got a response back from him...almost three pages single-spaced! Not thirty words or less. And in his three pages, he did a study on the Hebrew word 'steward' and gave a number of Biblical references and wrote that Jesus talked about the subject of money more than any other issue. And then at the end of his three pages he wrote, "I got you brother! You asked for thirty words or less and you got three pages. Just like God's generosity is for you and people of your church! And he showed that generosity through Jesus who is the true steward. If you want to study what it means to be a good steward, study Jesus."

Last week, as I was preparing for this Easter sermon, I called him again and asked, "What would you say to them on Easter?" He said to me, "What do you REALLY want to ask me? You can say it. It is OK". So I asked him what the real question on my mind was. "Luther, what would say to them on your LAST Easter on this earth?" He said to me, "Who is your audience? Describe to me your congregation." I began to give him a little description of who you were, age, places you work, your nitch here at Zion. He then said, "No I don't mean that." Let me tell you who will be your listener on Easter morning. You will have believers who have never doubted, and believers who have doubted, but believe most of the time. You will have doubters who have believed. And you will have doubters who have never believed, and don't plan on it...even regular church members. Some doubters and unbelievers will be in your church on Easter morning because it is the family thing to do. Some doubters and unbelievers are in church on Easter because they are looking for something that they are not getting in their lives and your members have invited them to look in your church. Some doubters and unbelievers will be in your church on Easter because the culture gives them permission to be here on this day like no other day. If you ask the doubters and unbelievers why they have never believed in the resurrection, you will soon discover that it is because they could not overcome the "Good Fridays" of their lives. "Pastor, I can't get past the sudden death of my mother"...A Good Friday. "Pastor, my husband's disease has been there for so long. Is there no hope? A Good Friday. Pastor, every hour of the day I can hear my loved one say, "I love you" and then she died. It just overcomes me"...another Good Friday.

In our text for this morning from John 20, Mary sat there grieving over her Good Friday, the death of Jesus. It overcame her. It overwhelmed her. It darkened her life. But then something happened. Jesus appeared, as he always does in the midst of the grief we face on our Good Fridays. And he began to talk to her but she did not recognize him. I always questioned that. How could she not recognize him? She even talked to him! She looked at him, but did not recognize him. The answer is, "She was overcome by her grief!" But then Jesus drove through her grief by calling her out by name, as he does to you and me, and said, "Mary." And she turned and saw who he was and went and told the disciples, "I have seen the Lord."

My friends, as we face our own Good Fridays, don't

be surprised if Jesus calls you by name, so tenderly, so compassionately. When He does, know that there is more to the story than our Good Fridays. Jesus rose from the dead allowing us to have a personal relationship with Him and in the midst of our darkest days, He calls each and every one of us by name and says to us, "I am alive and well in your life!"

And read the book, A SKEPTIC'S SEARCH FOR GOD by Ralph O. Muncaster. He tells the story of growing up in a Christian home and later in life becoming an atheist.

"Who would imagine that three boys, raised with 4368 hours of Sunday School and church teaching between them, would turn into hard-core atheists and agnostics only a few years later?" (p. 11) Muncaster goes on to tell how he became a Bible-basher and used many situations to try and disprove Christianity. He laughed at Christians and made fun of them. But something kept gnawing at him. Something kept him skeptical of atheism! And he discovered what it was... the resurrection! That was the piece of Christianity that gave him peace in the midst of his chaos and confusion. And once he accepted what Jesus did for him, his life was changed and be began to truly care about people, not just things.

Now back to Pastor Luther. I then asked him, "Who then should I preach to...the believers who have never doubted, or the believers who have doubted, but believe most of the time. Or the doubters who have believed and the doubters who have never believed and do plan on it?" Luther paused and said, "Preach to my wife Sarah, and my son, Ben and my daughter, Amy, call them individually by name, those who will soon face the Good Friday of their lives in the death of their husband and father. Imagine, on Easter morning, preaching from your pulpit, with no one else in the pews except Sarah, Amy and Ben. And know that they are sitting there begging for hope in their lives...hope to overcome their Good Friday. If you can do that, just preaching to them, you will catch the attention of ALL doubters and ALL believers and ALL unbelievers. Once you do that, tell your congregation this. (He told me to tell you to write this one down) "When I close my eyes on this earth to my family on MY Good Friday, I will again open them immediately to Jesus," and "I am at my best when I am linked to Jesus!"

My friends in Christ, Easter is more than celebrating the resurrection of Jesus from the dead...It is more than a day when WE mock death...It is more than the flowers and music...It is more than shouting HE IS RISEN, HE IS RISED INDEED. For Easter is the beginning of a new life for you and me LINKED to Jesus Christ. It is the day when we again are re-assured that our sins have been destroyed at the cross and we can live as forgiven people. The hope we leave with today, being a believer or not, is that "nothing will be able to separate us from the love of Christ. Not tribulation, or distress, or persecution, or famine, or nakedness, or peril or sword. Neither death, nor life, nor angels, nor principalities, nor things present, nor things to come, no powers, nor height, nor depth, nor anything else in all of creation, will be able to separate us from the love of God in Jesus Christ our Lord". Folks, that is the rest of the story for your lives!

Did the sermon connect with you this morning? I hope and pray that it did. But know that I preached it FOR Sarah, Amy and Ben. And remember, "Write this one down," "When I close my eyes on this earth to my family, on my Good Friday, I will again open them immediately to Jesus. And "You will be at your best when you are linked with the one who was raised from the dead, Jesus Christ." Amen

Chapter 23

The Grand Finale

"For Jesus said to her, 'I am the resurrection and the
life; he who believes in Me will live even if he dies and
everyone who lives and believes in Me will never die.'
Do you believe this?"
John 11:25-26

My mom, Bonnie Bauerle, wrote this story. As I re-read it again and again, I marvel at her gift. She has quite a faith story herself. In her lifetime she has lost her first child as an infant; her husband after a long illness; her youngest child with cystic fibrosis at the age of 43 and she is about to lose her son-in-law. She knows the pain and heartache of death and yet her heart and soul are filled with the love of Jesus. So, you see, she also knows her God is in control and that those she has loved so deeply in this life are with the same loving God she will live with eternally in the next life. Her story of death knocking at Luther's door is beautiful and filled with love. I thank her for this love of Christ she and my dad passed on to me.

Written by my mom, Bonnie Bauerle

Quite some time ago, Luther began a journey that ultimately brought us to this day. It was not an easy journey. Actually, it started out as a "fight" and then as many fights do it became a "battle" and then an "all-out battle."

He did not wage this battle alone…most battles involve many…the willing and the unwilling. Mostly it included Sarah, Amy and Ben as they helped fight this battle on a daily basis. In the beginning none of them were very good fighters though they knew a few basic strategies. However, as the time wore on, their skills were sharpened and they became wizened fighters… willing, but at the same time, not really wanting to fight.

As time wore on and the battle worsened and became threatening, they all realized they were not alone in this battle, nor had they ever been…family, mother, brothers, sister, friends, churches, communities…King of Kings… all joined the battle cry and the thoughts and prayers for Luther became legion.

As we came to the past few weeks and days, the battle raged and all joined together to bring Luther, Sarah, Amy and Ben through to safety. It was a tough fight and some times they seemed to gain ground…and then in a moment, they lost ground. But the fight continued.

From the earliest days of this battle, Luther, Sarah, Amy and Ben understood they needed Great Help and so began another journey…with Jesus , the Holy Spirit, and God Almighty…it would take all Three Persons to fight this battle.

Finally they all arrived close to the end of the battle. And one day recently, Death came to the door, knocking lightly…Death had an assignment…Death was calling for Luther. But we all know Luther…he would not go to the door. But death was persistent…Death had a job to do. Luther also understood this would be his greatest battle. He fought the good fight with all he had...and he had plenty...he had Sarah, Ben and Amy and a host of others on his side...especially he had Jesus, the Holy Spirit and God Almighty at his side.

Death and Luther began this battle...sometimes it seemed Death would gain ground and get in the door... sometimes Luther would appear to be winning. This battle gained momentum until the last few days when it was a great storm. Death kept appearing at the door, knocking...but the knocking became more intense, until the last few days when Death beat at Luther's door. Luther raged and roared, but would not open the door. Then I looked...and there was Luther...and he was not alone...there was Jesus! Both were beaten, bloodied and broken, holding back Death...Jesus had been in that battle all along.

Finally...finally, the battle was over...look at Luther and Jesus...Luther is smiling...and would you look at that, they are high-fiving and slapping each other on the back...and they are howling with laughter. Well, they surely must be the victors!!!

But Luther is weak...the battle has been tough. Look there...Jesus is now reaching out to Luther and gently enfolding him to His Bosom...Luther is still smiling... Now Jesus is tucking Luther into His sweet, everlasting arms. Sarah, Amy and Ben, do you see it????? Wait a minute, there is a whimpering and a gentle knock at the door...you see, Death no longer has any sting... But Death has come to complete his assignment...Jesus looks at the door...Luther is now quiet and at peace, safe in the everlasting arms of Jesus...and now, FINALLY...

finally, LIFE and LOVE answer the door.

Love, Mom

The vigil was continuing. Family and friends were in and out all day. The love in the room was abundant and there was a part of me that wondered if Luther would ever die. He had hung on for so long, passing all expectations of how long he could continue in this state. We continued reading the long list of Bible verses he had requested. I told Kim in the morning, "You know, Kim, he isn't going to let go until we get through ALL the list of verses." So for the next hour and a half she read to him, finishing up the list. How faithful.

Later that evening, at 6:30 p.m., we were expecting our music director, Ed Dawson, from our previous congregation, Truth Lutheran Church, to come over with his keyboard to sing some of our favorite songs. He had invited a few members of the choir to come and help make a joyful noise. Ed and one of the Truth members could always be counted on to be a little late. One of the miracles that day was that they were both right on time. I was finishing up a much needed shower and getting ready for the evening when David approached me and very tenderly said, "Sarah, it will be any minute now. His breathing is labored." All of a sudden I wasn't ready. Here we had been waiting for this moment and I wasn't ready.

All of Luther's loved ones gathered together, Toby, our black lab 'love dog' as we call him, took his place nearest Luther. There we were waiting for his last breath I watched…inhale…pause…exhale. Another inhale, slower…weaker…watching…waiting…waiting…

David began praying with a loud, trembling voice with a passion I had never heard before. "Dear Lord let your servant and child enter into your presence' …waiting…no breath. I cried out to David with what almost seemed like panic, 'David, is this it? Is that his last breath? Are you sure?' With his loving hands on my shoulders, Amy and Ben on either side of Luther, crying…there was crying… Amy and Ben…He was gone. At that moment, Ed began playing Holy Ground and those in the room began singing. I remember the beauty of their voices. They sounded like angels. I am certain they were. After some time, I asked everyone else to leave the room so Amy, Ben and I could have time alone with their Dad, just us. There we were. Alone with Luther. The heartbreak of hearing their cries. As we sat, the song I Can Stand, by Kirk Franklin, began to play. There I stood, able to touch Luther and Amy and Ben all at the same time singing the words: I know I can stand. With Jesus I know I can make it… The words came from my heart and I was filled with hope. So much hope. I knew that as Luther closed his eyes on this earth, he opened them to see his God and Savior. My heart was bursting with joy, love, and thankfulness. Everyone had a chance to spend time with Luther to say their good byes. I will always cherish that time. Meanwhile, in downtown Lake Orion it was the July 4th fireworks celebration. Church members and friends lived downtown and always had a huge party. The year Luther was diagnosed the firework celebration and party were underway and an announcement was made of Luther's illness. On this night, the message of Luther's death was also announced. I can only imagine their reaction and response. We always marvel at this 'coincidence'. It was about midnight when friends began arriving from the firework celebration. I am not sure who all was there when they took Luther out for the last time but I felt their love and presence of God.

I often wondered with trepidation how this day and time would come. I should have known God's plan was a finale grander than Hollywood. What God had done for me and my children that day, that hour, that minute no words can begin to express. Love, love, love. Thank you my sweet Jesus.

I sit here at 1:50 a.m. not sure if sleep will come tonight. Luther died at 6:37 p.m.; very quietly and with many people in the room. We were able to sit with him for a long time before we called Hospice to come. They arrived and the sheriff came since he died at home and then the funeral home came about one hour later. That was probably the hardest because I knew that once he left the house he was gone. He is going to be cremated. Amazingly enough he died two years to the minute that we found out about the cancer. So our bedroom is quiet. I had the hospital bed removed before I went back there because I thought it would be tough to go in there and see his bed empty. My heart aches and I am not quite sure what to do at this point. We have prayed a lot and shared stories, but there are still those alone moments that somehow I am to adjust to. Ben asked how long this feeling would last. Too bad I had no answer except that no matter how long, Jesus is there, watching and protecting. For that I am grateful.

I thank you for your continued prayers and ask that they continue. Much love to you all,

Sarah

Chapter 24

The Race is Won

"However, I consider my life worth nothing to me, if
only I may finish the race and complete the task the
Lord Jesus has given me-the task of testifying to
the gospel of God's grace."
Acts 20:24

We come to the end of Luther's journey in this life. I
find it bittersweet. There is great sadness at this point, July
3, 2004 and the continued journey to this day. Sometimes
the wound of Luther being gone is unbearable, but I am
continually reminded of where he is now. He is gone from
my life physically, but he is now in the very presence of
God. The creator of all, the God Luther loves so. The God
that saves us from our sin. The same God who holds and
loves Luther is the same God who holds and loves me.

In this last email I share my struggles in the days
after the funeral.

July 8, 2004

*Here it is Thursday, July 8, 2004. All of the rushing
around is done. People are beginning to head home and
things to settle down. Kind of a scary feeling, I must
admit. The visitation was wonderful and the people and*

the love present were so uplifting. Luther was really something and people have been so good to tell me how he touched their lives. The hugs and kisses were comforting. Thank you. I felt very tired that night and thought sleep would come easily but I was somewhat mistaken. It was late when I got to bed and then about 3:00 a.m., I woke up and my mind began racing about details and things to do before the funeral. All of which was taken care of by many people. I finally realized I was going to my husband's funeral in a few hours and I guess this is pretty normal for such an upcoming day. I came into the living room and after some time I was able to rest in the chair. It was an emotional morning. Getting to the church and waiting for things to begin was difficult. Walking in I was wondering if I was going to be able to get through this. But then Dr. Featherstone (Rudy) began to speak and I felt the Spirit and I was instantly uplifted and touched. The day was glorious. Jesus was present and celebrated as Luther wanted and the Resurrection was the theme of the day. Praise God!!! Looking around at all of the people and listening to the singing and hearing Rudy's sermon, all was good and at times felt entirely filled with joy that only comes from my God who provides all that is needed. As the service came to an end I did feel a sense of uncertainty. What will be happening in the next days and weeks when all is quiet and life goes back to "normal"? I remembered, the same God who was present with us during Luther's illness and surely these last days. He showed Himself so clearly and will continue to hold Amy, Ben and I very close. I do trust those loving arms and I think I will place myself and my children safely there.

How do I begin to thank all of you for your goodness, love, compassion, watchfulness, food, prayers, love, mercy, tenderness, oh and did I mention love? Luther is now with his Creator whom he both loved and adored. How magnificent. I will continue to Trust Only Jesus Always for He is my Rock and my comfort. Why would I trust anything else? I miss Luther so much already and miss being able to touch him and I am sure that will be there for a long, long time. He did remind me at Christmas that he is my one true love and I am his one true love. For now, my love to all of you and please continue your prayers and I will continue to watch for God's mighty hand, love, grace and mercy day to day.

Love, Sarah

I find it interesting how Satan tries to come in and "change" my heart; confuse my thinking. Then I am reminded whose I am and that God is in charge of all of this: my life, my children's life, my church's life. A few days after Luther died, I found myself lost. I worried that Luther was as lost as me. Was he in Heaven? Really? Was God taking care of him? Was his pain gone or was he still suffering? As I have lost loved ones in the past, I never had these thoughts. I felt guilty. I felt paralyzed. Why with the death of my husband was I feeling unconvinced? I then called my sister-in-law, Carol Ann and told her I wanted to thank David and Don for the tender love and care they gave Luther. I was trying to express my feelings about that love and care and told her of my feeling lost and confused. As we spoke she told me that during the coma week, what we saw and experienced was the very love of God. That was the only way to express it. All of a sudden, the light went on and the dark cloud of doubt was lifted. I laughed out loud (again) and told her that a God who can provide such tender love before our death surely can and does provide even a greater love after death… in Heaven. I have not felt the doubt or confusion since. I am also convinced that Luther is without pain and feels a love greater then my human self can even begin to imagine. I may not understand cancer and Luther dying at age 45, BUT I know God is God and He has it all under control. Again I am reminded that I can trust the one who bled and died for me on the cross. He is Risen! He is Risen indeed!

I often think about –daydream-what it will be like when Luther and I see each other again. I was thinking of a time before Luther and I were married, the summer between our junior and senior years in college. He was at home in Florida and I was at home in Ohio. We spoke everyday on the phone. He was coming up for a visit in July. My brother and his fiancée took me to the airport to pick him up. When he came off the plane and we saw each other: "The Look." Our eyes locked, so thrilled to see each other, to be able to touch each other. It was intense and seemed to last forever, like we could see into each other's hearts. And then, he kissed me. Heavenly! That is what it will be like. Being apart and then reunited. He will look at me with those same loving, gentle, intense eyes. We will be together again. My brother told me later that it gave him chills to witness our reunion. He saw our connection that night. Thank you Jesus for the time you did give me with Luther. By the way, those eyes, "The Look", the love in them, I saw many times in our years together. What we had was so special and a gift from God.

Luther lived for God, running the race God put before him. His example of trusting only Jesus always and loving all who knew him and all God brought across his path left everyone covered with the love of God. It left each of us changed by his great example. You see, in the end, Luther didn't get a new liver or new shoes, but he did win the race set out for him. Because in the end it's not about what you get in this world it's about what you leave behind. Thank you Luther!!! Thank you God!!!...Still trusting...Always!!!

Overflowing in God's Love, Sarah

Ben on the beach

Epilogue

Luther had a gift of being able to put all in the Lord's hands. Throughout this journey God placed before us what we needed to read and hear. He placed people in our lives to lift us up and to show Himself clearly through their love. My faith at the beginning of this journey was the size of a mustard seed. Today it is deeper, bolder, and stronger. That does not mean I do not have doubts or confusion or sadness or despair. It means, now in those moments, I know where to go and who to call on. I call on the One who never forsakes me and the One who carried the heavy cross, hung upon it and died for me. I call on the One who snatched victory from the evil one on that first Easter morning. I call on the One whose name is Jesus. Ah, Jesus. He is there for you, too.

If you've never asked Jesus into you heart I can't think of a better time than now. Romans 10:13 tells us "for, Everyone who calls on the name of the Lord will be saved." Come to God as a little child and confess Jesus as your Lord by praying this prayer:

Heavenly Father, I believe in my heart that Jesus hung on the cross, shed His blood, and died for me. I believe that Jesus is Your Son and that you raised Him from the dead, where He is seated at Your right hand. Today, I confess aloud with my mouth that Jesus is Lord of all, and I am asking Jesus to be the Lord of my life. I believe I am born anew. Amen

Welcome into the Lord's family. Look for a church that will support your relationship with God and to be a part of His amazing family of love.

Thanks for sharing this journey with me.

The Miracle of the Sevens…

Seven is the perfect number in the Bible, meaning completeness. It is the number used to represent Jesus (perfect and complete). These are just some of the '7's I noticed along the way.

7 weeks / Luther had no food yet sustained by God's Word.
7 days / no fluid
Diagnosed 7/3/2002
Died 7/3/2004 –The three represents the Trinity: Father, Son and Holy Spirit.
 Ben's baseball number was #3
Died at 6:37pm
Eulogy verse Isaiah 63:7chosen by Luther weeks before
Funeral 7/7
7 years later, after Luther's death, this book will be published.

Streams in the Desert
L.B. Cowman
Zondervan Publishing
1997

Grace for the Moment
Max Lucado
J. Countryman Publishing
2000

Purpose Driven Church
Rick Warren
Zondervan Publishing
1995

The Blood of Christ
Andrew Murray
Bethany House Publishing
Minneapolis, MN
2001

African American Pulpit
Spring 1999
"Resurrection Means Peace'

Touch the Top of the World
Erik Weihenmayer
Penguin Publishing
2002

Bird by Bird: Some Instructions on Writing and Life
Story told by Jack Cornfield

Recorded by Anne Lamott
Anchor Books
1995

Speaking of Trust: Conversing with Luther about the
Sermon on the Mount
Martin Marty
Augsburg Fortress Press.
2003

I Can Stand
Kirk Franklin/Nu Nation

A Speptic's Seareh for God
Ralph O. Muncaster
Harvest House Publishing
2002

10708617R00136

Made in the USA
Charleston, SC
26 December 2011